The WORLD Through My Eyes

THE TRUTH KEEPERS OF THE SACRED
MIRROR MIRROR...

About this book

In this book you will discover many hidden truths in plain sight. You will venture down a road that you never knew existed. I can only offer you the truth and nothing but the truth. I can't tell you what that truth is however, but I can show you the door, for it is up to you if you the reader, the traveler to walk through that door I am providing. It has taken me well over fifth teen years to compile all this information. I believe with great power comes great responsibility! I was told that this is an impossible dream of mine. How can that be when we all dream? I was told that I was too out there in my thinking about the way I perceive things. I was told it couldn't be done. That is all fine and well until it is done! I only see I'm possible in that word, not the other way around. I do hope this enlightens you and makes you more aware of what you are capable of achieving, believing and doing while you are here. You matter, I matter, and we all do. You have a right to be here, I have that right too. I have that right to share my continue knowledge on this journey through life. I do hope that you find this to be a pleasant read. I hope you take a bit of me with you in your heart. I hope that you can change your life and better your future! It all begins with us. I want to take that first step, and it being me.

Table of contents:

About Book – 3 &4
Table of Contents - 5-12
Believe – In the power of you - 13
Electric Eyes – Windows the soul - 14
Death & Rebirth - 15
3rd Eye – Tuning in - 16
Orichalcum – Metal antiquity – 17-18
Atlantis – New Discoveries - 19
Pyramid – Torsion Waves – 20-21
The Spiral - 22
The Cross of Atlantis - 23
The symbols of Atlantis - 24
Triquetra Symbol - 25
The Ancient Symbol - 26
Antahkarana - 27

The Record Keepers - 28

Paradise or Mind's Eye - 29

The Pineal Gland - 30

Fluoride – Water supply – 31-32

Triskelion Symbol - 33

Pine cone – Related to the Pineal Gland – 34

Calcification of the Pineal Gland -35

Boost your Pineal Gland – 36-37

GMO's – Monsanto and other toxins -37-38

Glyphosate & pesticide list - Food control – 39

Worsen the modern disease – 40

Glyphosate kills - 41

Monsanto established – 42

Trade secrets – 43-44

Agent Orange & and Dixon and its effects – 44-46

Food Labeling Act – 47– 48

Glyphosate chart - 49

Monsanto kills chart – 50

You don't want to miss - GMO's - 51

The help - 52

Babylon - 53

Epicyte - 54

The Laws - 55

Money & Profits – Corporate Globalization – 56-57

Pesticides – Listing – 58-59

3rd Eye – We're powerful - 60

Other side - 61

Drop in an ocean- 62

Peacock Ore - 63

Puzzle Pieces - 64
Neuroplasticity – Cerebral Cortex -65
Left side Vs Right side - 66
Wired – Circuit running - 67
Glial Cells – Einstein Vs Tesla – 68-71
The Mind is God – 72 -73
Flames – The balance - 74
Rainbow – Charka energy centers -75
Violet Flame - 76
The World in your hands - 77
Energy sent out - 78
Healing hands - 79
Energy focus - 80
Finding truth – Your truth - 81
Earth Love - 82
Quantum energy - 83
Gravitational waves - 84

Cern – LHC – 84

Rising Frequencies – 85-87

Heirloom – Mitochondrial - Cytochrome – DNA- 88

Stimulating Cell Growth – STR1 - 89

Resveratrol chart - 90

Resveratrol – Increases UVB protection - 91

Amino Acids – Listing – 92

Body's Ph – Chart and listings – 93

Cell salts – 94 -96

A quick fix – 97

Spiritual warfare chart - 98

Chakras & Stones - 99

Chakra Chart - 100

7 Chakra Food Chart – 101

Something cracks – 102 -103

Worldly hands – 104
Meditation – 105
Take a little trip – 106
The blueprint – 107
Your thoughts – 108 – 109
All life – 110 – 112
The mirror – 113
The vortex – Ascension – 114
Female VS Male energies chart -115
Energy breaks-down – 116
Each soul & repression - 117
Humanity rising - 118
Prop 37 chart – 119
Kundalini rising chart – 120
Kundalini crown -121
Love beings with me - 122
I have a dream – 123

The key to light – 124
Ocean star – 125
The lion awakens – 126
Universal Love – 127
The secret – 128
The merkaba – 129
All matter exist – 130
The tri-spiral – 131
Me – 132
Investing in our future – 133
Guardian Angel – 134
Starseed awakening – 135
Nicolas Telsa – Frequencies – 136
Genius periodic table – 137
Goddess rising pictures – 138
Goddess defined – 139 – 140
Goddess picture & The Divine – 140

U-verse art piece -141--142

Books to come – 143-146

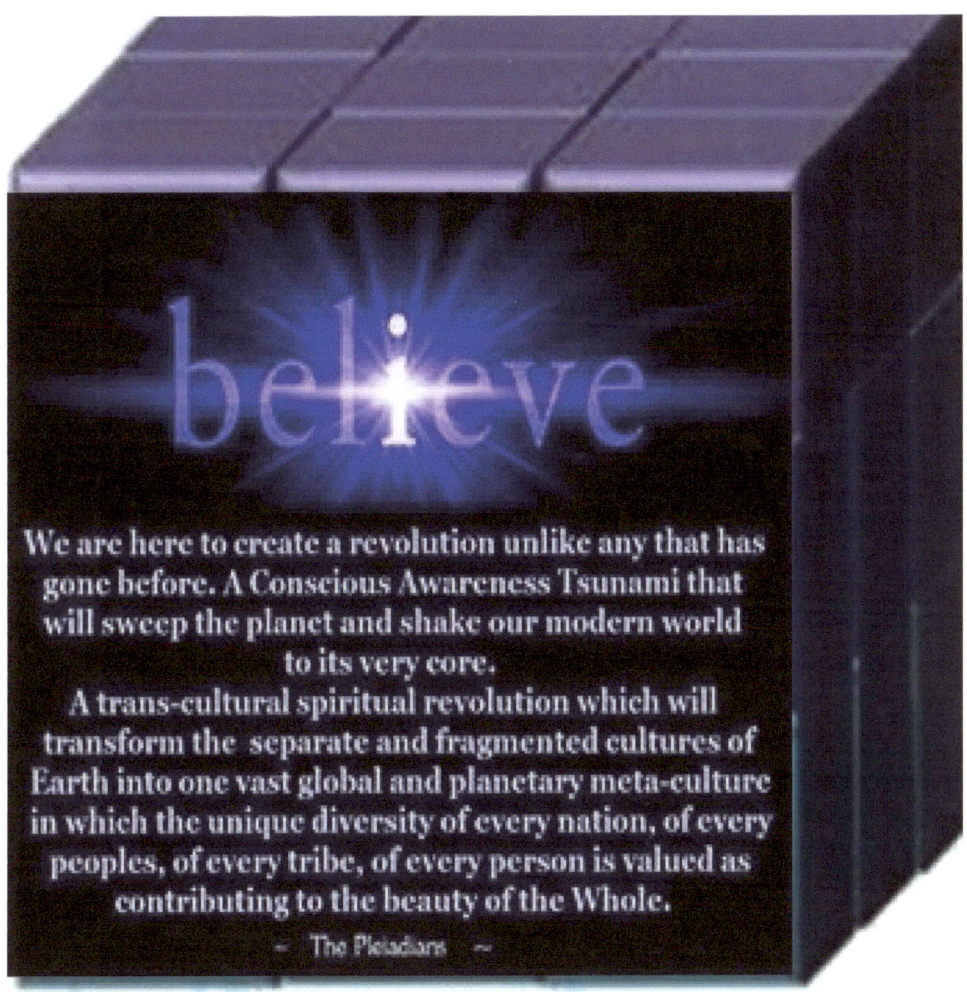

The WORLD Through My Eyes. Copyright 2016 by Aprile Plummer.
This book author retains sole copyrights to his or her contributions to this book.
ISBN# 978-069-2733394

Electric Eyes – Your eyes are the windows to your soul. What does it say about you?

Death & rebirth = **LIFE** + **TIME** = **INFINITY**. We're Infinite beings of life. What you choose to do with it is entirely up to you.

Tune in, tune up and turn on your light. How else are you to reach your highest level of spiritual awareness and enlightenment? Get some sun, this helps turn on your **3rd eye.**

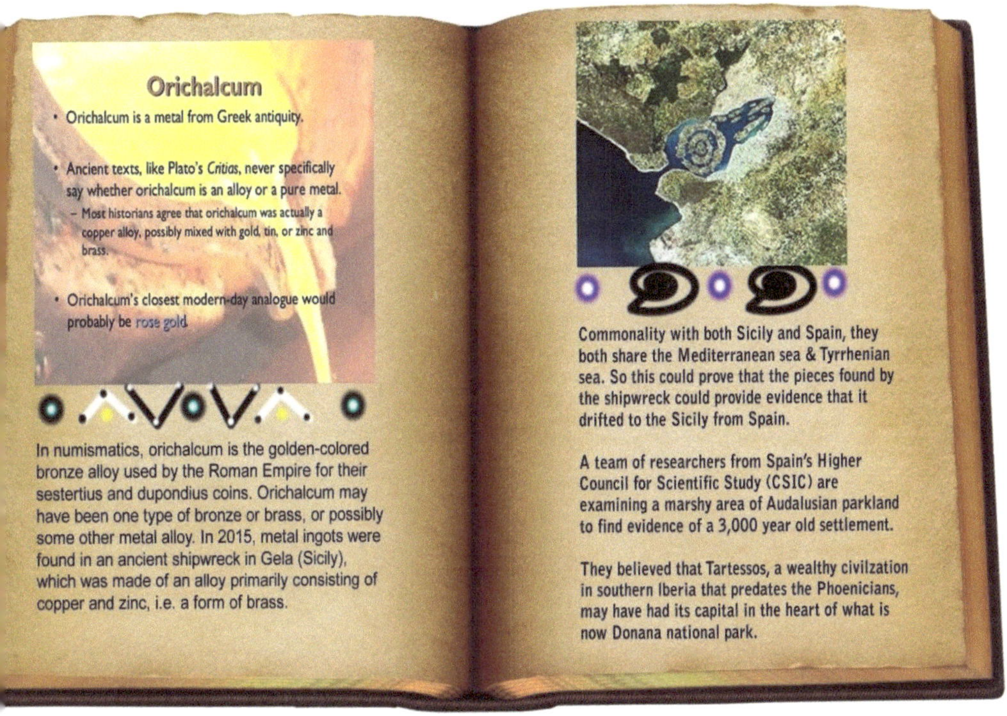

Orichalcum

- Orichalcum is a metal from Greek antiquity.

- Ancient texts, like Plato's *Critias*, never specifically say whether orichalcum is an alloy or a pure metal.
  - Most historians agree that orichalcum was actually a copper alloy, possibly mixed with gold, tin, or zinc and brass.

- Orichalcum's closest modern-day analogue would probably be rose gold.

In numismatics, orichalcum is the golden-colored bronze alloy used by the Roman Empire for their sestertius and dupondius coins. Orichalcum may have been one type of bronze or brass, or possibly some other metal alloy. In 2015, metal ingots were found in an ancient shipwreck in Gela (Sicily), which was made of an alloy primarily consisting of copper and zinc, i.e. a form of brass.

Commonality with both Sicily and Spain, they both share the Mediterranean sea & Tyrrhenian sea. So this could prove that the pieces found by the shipwreck could provide evidence that it drifted to the Sicily from Spain.

A team of researchers from Spain's Higher Council for Scientific Study (CSIC) are examining a marshy area of Audalusian parkland to find evidence of a 3,000 year old settlement.

They believed that Tartessos, a wealthy civilzation in southern Iberia that predates the Phoenicians, may have had its capital in the heart of what is now Donana national park.

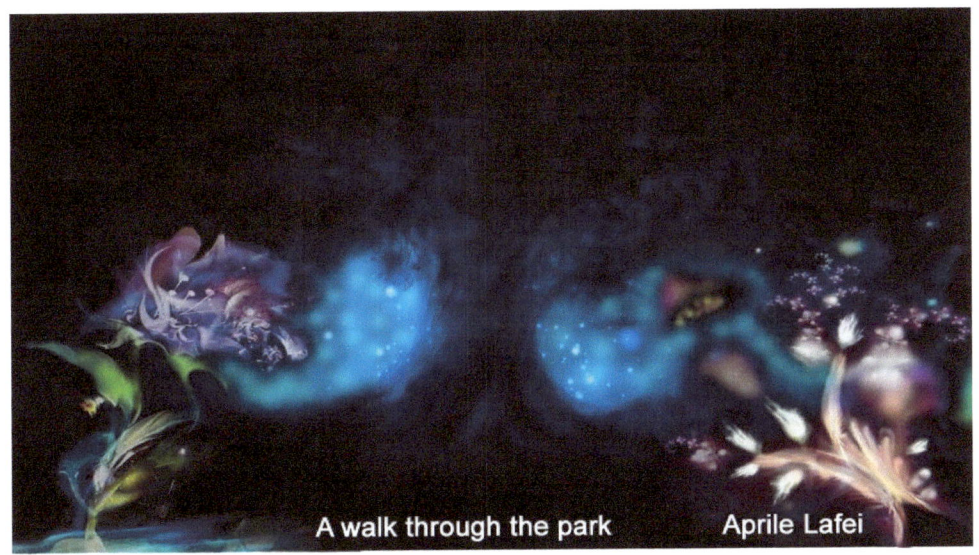

A walk through the park — Aprile Lafei

According to the ancient Greeks, it was invented by Cadmus, a Greek-Phoenician mythological character. The fourth century B.C. Greek philosopher Plato made orichalcum a legendary metal when he mentioned it in the Critias dialogue. Gleaming cast metal called orichalcum, which was said by Ancient Greeks to be found in Atlantis, has been recovered from a ship that sank 2,600 years ago off the coast of Sicily. The lumps of metal were arriving to Gela in southern Sicily, possibly coming from Greece or Asia Minor. The ship that was carrying them was likely caught in a storm and sunk just when it was about to enter the port. "The wreck dates to the first half of the sixth century," Sebastian Tusa, Sicily's superintendent of the Sea Office, told Discovery News. "It was found about 1,000 feet from Gela's coast at a depth of 10 feet."

Atlantis – New Discoveries

Until now historians had dismissed the region as a possible site believing that it had been submerged since the ice age. But it is claimed new evdience suggests the waters may have receded in time for the Tartessians to build an urban centre, which was later destoryed in a tsunami.

The Hinojos marshes, an area close to the mouth of the Guadalquiver River where it meets the Atlantic, have now been pinpointed as the site most likely to provide evidence of a lost city.

Archaeological findings have already proved the existence of Tartessians culture at sites on the opposite bank of the river.

Plato wrote that the city of Atlantis was a known naval power that had conquered many parts of Europe and Africa, but failed to invade Athens. It was thought to have existed around 9600 BC. Plato wrote that Atlantis sank into the ocean. "in a single day and night of misfortune." Excavations will be continuing and already have the World's attention. Describing Atlantis as flashing. "with the red light of the orichalcum, he wrote that the metal, second only in value to gold, was mined in the mythical island and was used to cover Poseidon's temple interior walls, columns and floors." Today most scholars agree orichalcum is brass-like alloy, which was made in antiquity by cementation. This process was achieved with the reaction of zinc ore, charcoal and copper metal in a crucible. Analyzed with X-ray fluorescence by Dario Panetta, of TQ - Technologies for quality, the 39 ingots turned to be an alloy made with 75-80 percent copper, 15-20 percent zinc and small percentages of nickel, lead and iron. According to the scholar, who claimed in his book "journey to the Mythological Inferno" that the aNcient Greeks had discovered America, a "metallic alloy with fire-like reflections" similarto Plato's description was found in a set of metallic jaguars of Chavin style, which turned to be made of 9 percent copper, 76 percent gold and 15 percent silver. He noted that the 39 ingots found on the sand floor represent a unique finding."Nothing similar has ever been found, Tusa said. "We knew orichalcum from ancient texts and a few ornamntal objects." Indeed orichalcum has long been considered a mysterious metal, its composition and origin widely debated.

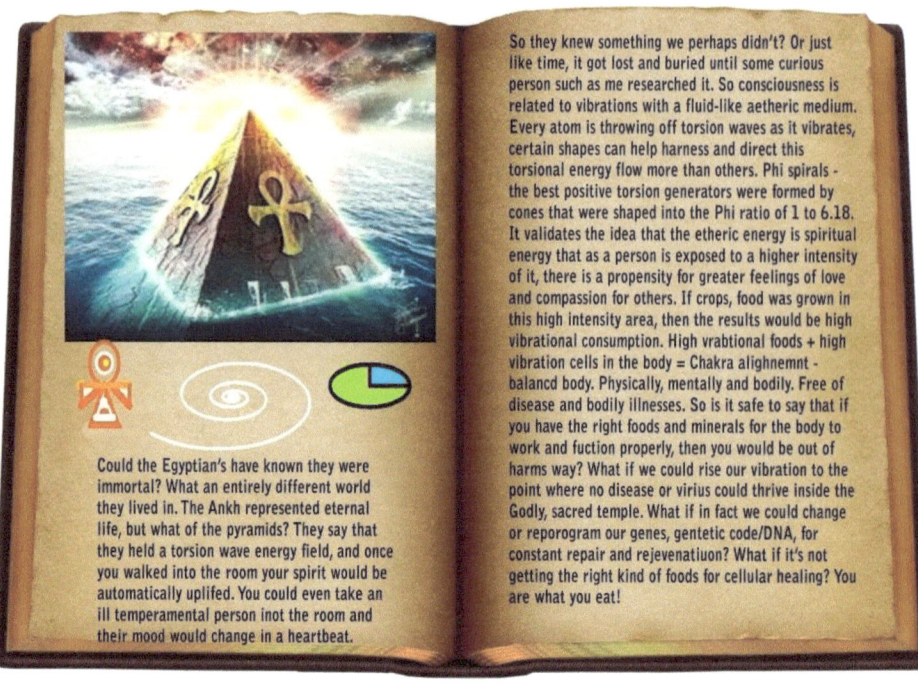

Could the Egyptian's have known they were immortal? What an entirely different world they lived in. The Ankh represented eternal life, but what of the pyramids? They say that they held a torsion wave energy field, and once you walked into the room your spirit would be automatically uplifed. You could even take an ill temperamental person inot the room and their mood would change in a heartbeat.

So they knew something we perhaps didn't? Or just like time, it got lost and buried until some curious person such as me researched it. So consciousness is related to vibrations with a fluid-like aetheric medium. Every atom is throwing off torsion waves as it vibrates, certain shapes can help harness and direct this torsional energy flow more than others. Phi spirals - the best positive torsion generators were formed by cones that were shaped into the Phi ratio of 1 to 6.18. It validates the idea that the etheric energy is spiritual energy that as a person is exposed to a higher intensity of it, there is a propensity for greater feelings of love and compassion for others. If crops, food was grown in this high intensity area, then the results would be high vibrational consumption. High vrabtional foods + high vibration cells in the body = Chakra alighnemnt - balancd body. Physically, mentally and bodily. Free of disease and bodily illnesses. So is it safe to say that if you have the right foods and minerals for the body to work and fuction properly, then you would be out of harms way? What if we could rise our vibration to the point where no disease or virius could thrive inside the Godly, sacred temple. What if in fact we could change or reporgram our genes, gentetic code/DNA, for constant repair and rejevenatiuon? What if it's not getting the right kind of foods for cellular healing? You are what you eat!

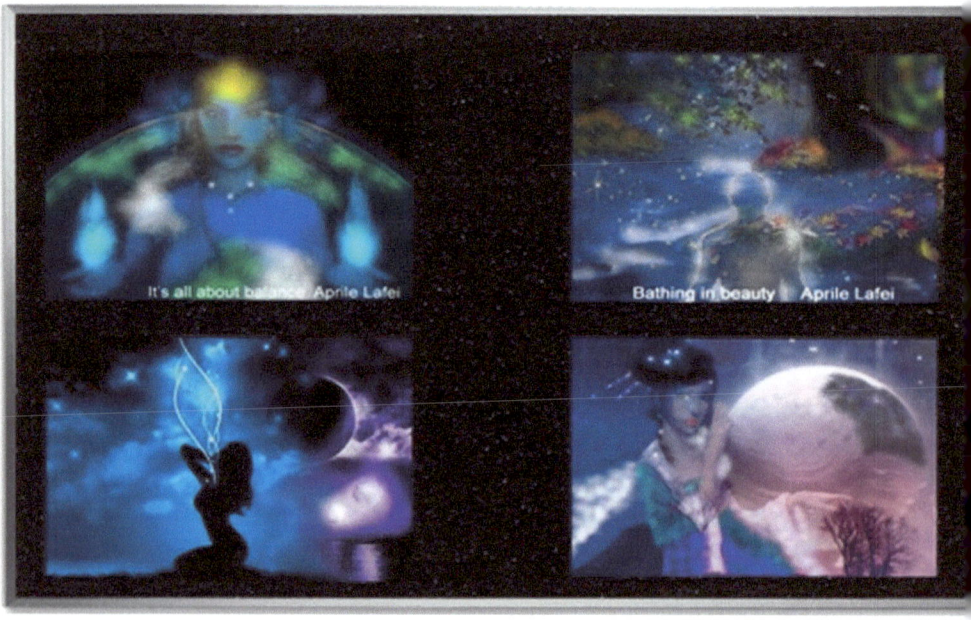

Using the latest sonar technology, satellite photography and earth penetrating radar, scientists are fairly confident that the remains of Atlantis are to be found buried in Doñana National Park, in the province of Huelva Doñana National Park. Could the marshlands of Doñana National park hold the answer to a 9000 year old mystery? Scientists have identified a ring-like structure underground that could be the remains of Atlantis. The physical and historical evidence all points to a city that was destroyed thousands of years ago by a giant tsunami. Plato's early account. The scientific evidence is backed up by Plato's early account of Atlantis. The Greek philosopher Plato wrote "that Atlantis was an island that sat just in front of the 'Pillars of Hercules,' today known as the Strait of Gibraltar."

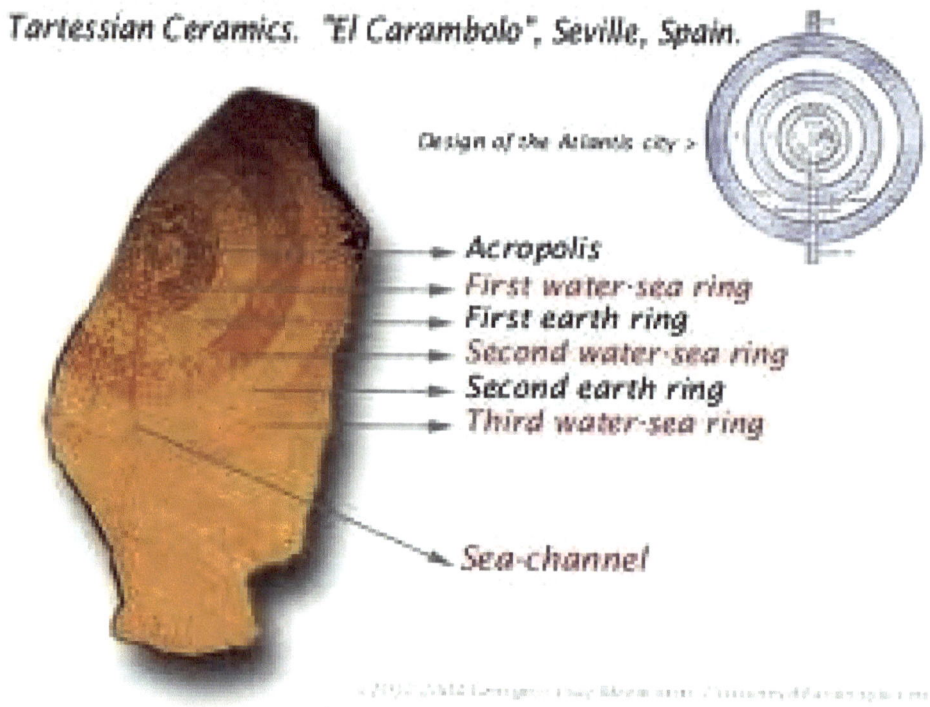

Tartessian Ceramics. "El Carambolo", Seville, Spain.

Design of the Atlantis city >

- Acropolis
- First water-sea ring
- First earth ring
- Second water-sea ring
- Second earth ring
- Third water-sea ring
- Sea-channel

Spiral - The Spiral, which is the oldest symbol known to be used in spiritual practices, reflects the universal pattern of growth and evolution. The spiral represents the goddess, the womb, fertility and life force energy. Reflected in the natural world, the Spiral is found in human physiology, plants, minerals, animals, energy patterns, weather, growth and death. The Spiral is a sacred symbol that reminds us of our evolving journey in life.

The Cross of Atlantis. The Atlantis logo is composed of a sun disk or Cross of Light in concentric rings. According to the Magdalene Legacy, A cross with a line going through it was called: Rosi-Crucis – The Dew Cup. It was the original symbol for the Holy Grail.

This is an ancient symbol dating back to Atlantis. This was a very powerful healing symbol that gives protection and help intuition.

The term **Triquetra** comes from Latin, and it means "three-cornered." There are many schools of thought when discussing the Celtic trinity knot meaning. All of the various interpretations agree on a culmination of thee parts. For example, early Christian understanding views the symbols as the Father, Son and Holy Spirit.

An ancient symbol known to go back to the days when Atlantis was said to exist. This was dating back to the Mystery Schools. They were very enlighten back then. They were known to have had very advanced technology and probably far beyond our current understanding of it. It wasn't until darkness took over and overthrew their people who knew this information/knowledge was lost. Maybe that is why they call it the lost city of Atlantis.

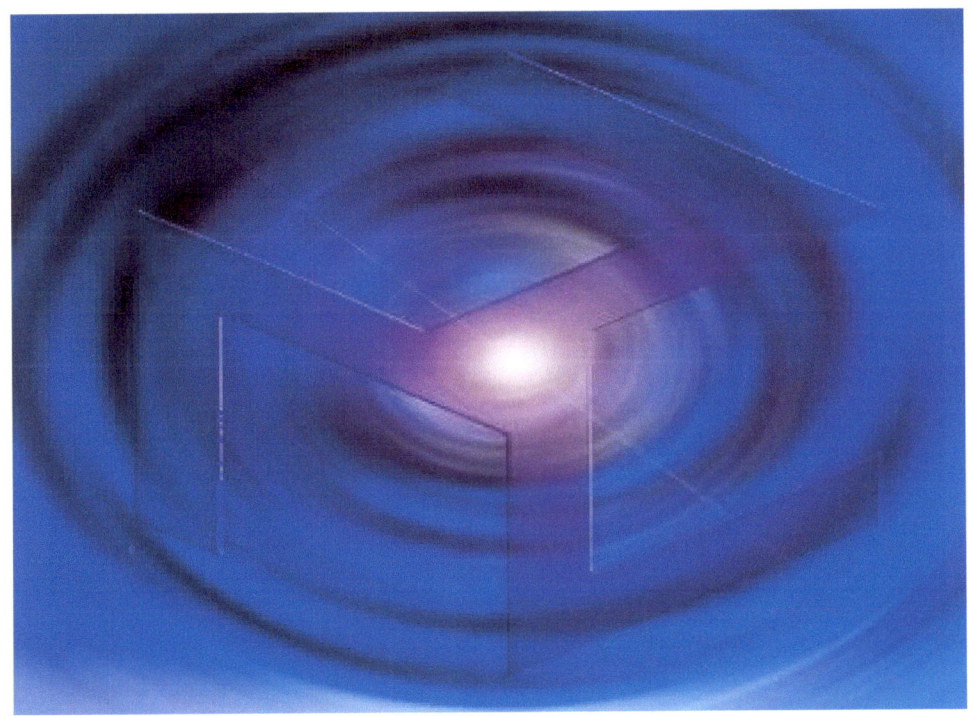

In Hindu philosophy, the **antahkarana** (Sanskrit: the inner cause) refers to the totality of two levels of mind, namely the Buddha, the intellect or higher mind, and the manas, the middle levels of mind which (according to theosophy) exist as or include the mental body.

Certainly the new found discoveries are enough to make you wonder about an ancient city full of higher vibrations, energy and most importantly healing. It surely makes you wonder why in some odd way we feel strangely connected to the past. It would be interesting and so soul rejuvenating to have been in this era. People seem friendlier and easier to get along with until the dark lords took over. The balance once again must be restored; God's light and children of the sun must rise again! The record keepers.

Is paradise a place or is it in the mind's eye? This highly evolved place seems to be something of a fairytale and yet it's somewhere in our psyche. Do we ever really get to experience this kind of living while we are here or is it just a dream within a dream? Dolphins are magical creatures, and they have the power to heal ones energy, chakras/aura. Try swimming with them while you are on Earth! You will notice a difference in your energy centers.

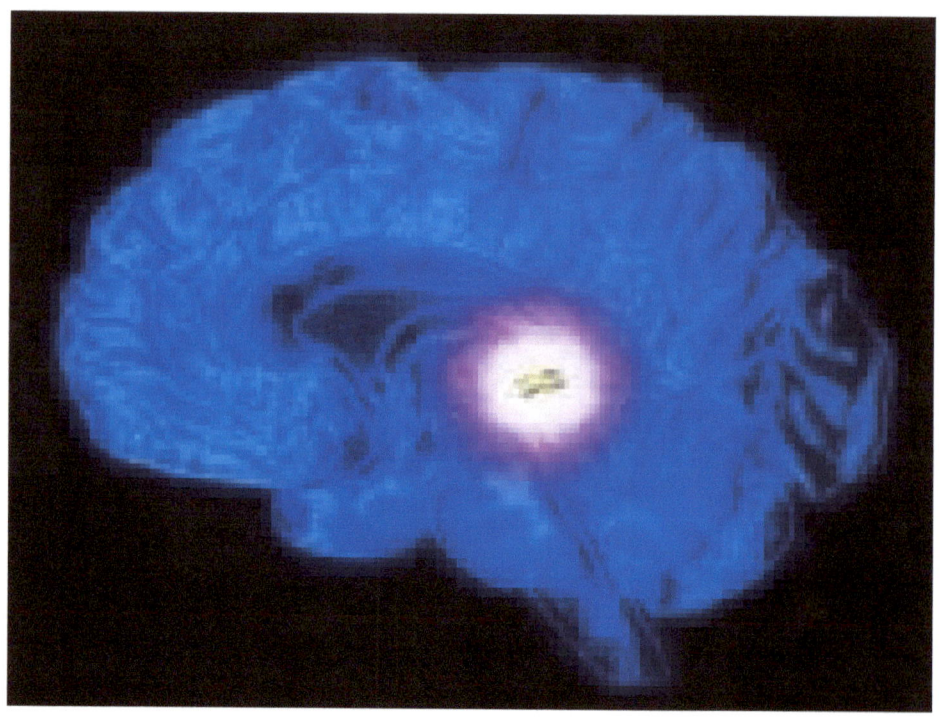

Pineal Gland, also known as the all "seeing eye" One of the biggest cover ups in human history. The secret that they don't want you to know. Everyone has a pineal gland, and it can be activated by spiritual practices, to spiritual world frequencies, that enable you to have a sense of all-knowing Godlike euphoria an oneness all around you. A pineal gland, once turned into the proper frequencies will help of meditation, yoga and other spiritual practices or various esoteric, occult methods, enabling one to travel to other dimensions otherwise known as astral travel or astral projection.

How are they killing your pineal gland you might ask? In the late 90's, a Scientist by the name of Jennifer Luke carries out first study the effects of Sodium Fluoride on the pineal gland. She determined that the pineal gland, located in the middle of the brain, was a target for fluoride. The Pineal Gland simply absorbed more fluoride than any physical matter in the body, even bones. Pineal Gland is a magnet to sodium fluoride. This calcifies the gland and makes it no longer effective in balancing the entire hormonal process through the body.

Fluoride is prevalent in foods, beverage and in our bath and drinking water. Sodium Fluoride is put in 90% of the United States drinking water supply. Water filters you buy don't take out the Fluoride. Only reverse Osmosis or water distillation.

Sodium fluoride is in our water supply, food, Pepsi, toothpaste, coke, to dumb down the mass, literally!

The fluoride was introduced into the water by the Nazis & Russian's in their concentration camps to make the camp population docile and do not question Authority. If you take away the seat of the soul, you take our oneness away with spirit & God, our source of spirituality and this turns us into mundane slaves, to Secret Societies, Shadow Governments, and Organizations. The control freak Corporate World. The function of the pineal gland – Produces Melatonin, which helps maintain circadian rhythm and regulate reproductive hormones. Smallest and most important endocrine glands.

Triskelion meaning as a Celtic Symbol: In short, the sum of this Celtic symbol meaning is: personal growth human development and spiritual expansion.

The pine cone dates back in ancient times and modern times as well. If you clearly look at the image you can see that on the staff there is a pine cone around the top portion. This is a representation of power, not only that but it is showing this is related to the pineal gland, that being the 3rd eye. "The spiritual eye" all beings have this. We seem to over time forget who we really are as a multi-dimensional being made from God. Because over time this is put to sleep by the food we consume, or just how we live our lifestyle in general. It's crazy to awake to this level of consciousness. It all makes sense though. The truth will always rise to the surface. Now more than ever people are seeking answers anywhere they can find them. The world is in the hands of wicked. This pine cone you see here is in the Vatican City. With it standing 13 ft t tall with two peacocks beside it. This is our birthright that has been taken from us! We are more than we realize. Wake up before it's too late. It stands for eternal life, as well as pine cones are from evergreen trees. This can be found at *Cortille Della Pigna at the Vatican Museum.*

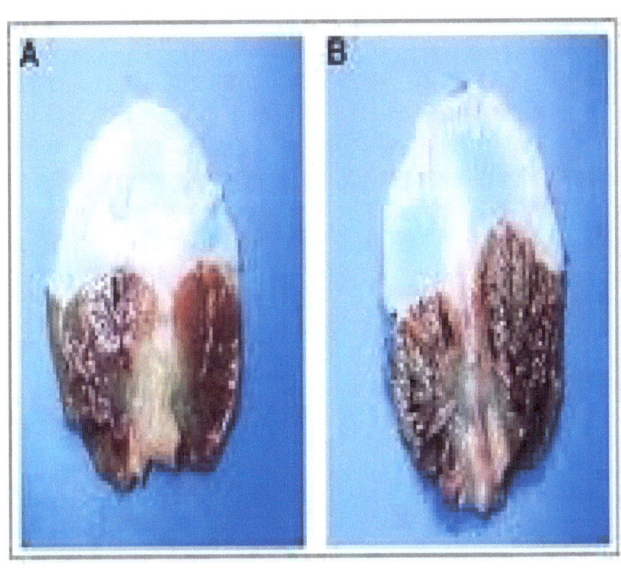

A pineal gland. Fluoride is deposited here as a result of consumption of fluoridated water.

Supplements to boost your pineal gland:
1. Melatonin
2. Oregano oil & Neem Extract
3. Raw Cacao
4. Chlorophyll – Rich Super foods
5. Raw Apple Cider Vinegar
6. Iodine
7. Organic Blue Ice Skate fish oil and Activator X (Vitamin K1/K2).
8. Boron/Borax

9. Other – Cilantro, Tamarid, Goji berries, watermelon, bananas, honey, coconut oil, hemp seeds, seaweed, noni juice, garlic, chaga mushroom, raw lemon juice. Alkaline foods.

What in the world is happening in our world today, let's take a look and see!

GMO'S- Monsanto – Glyphosate. Controlling the World Food Supply and the farmers.

So how is controlling the food supply you ask? Well no other than Monsanto, which now all foods are patent and protected by Monsanto, which I call Monsantan. I will go over this a bit more in a few. You now have to buy from them, and can't keep any seeds, as Monsanto hires detectives everywhere in the country. Engineered genes have a bad habit of turning up in Non-GE crops. And when this happens, sustainable farmers and their customers pay a high price. The farmers get contaminated by Monsanto, yet have to pay Monsanto all their year's crop or profit, even if there is no harvest yielded and even if they are contaminated by only 1%. It's certainly poison to us! You buy cheap food, you are what you eat! That is why it's very important to check the back of the label to know what you are consuming. I will further elaborate on the very damaging effects of Glyphosate –Roundup Ready, Agent Orange and Formaldehyde.

Ok, let's start with Glyphosate: is a broad-spectrum systemic herbicide and an organophosphorus compound, specifically a phosphosate. It's used to kill weeds, especially annual broadleaf weeds and grasses that compete with crops.

So now that we have this information pertaining to how it can ultimately affect our health. Roundup, which is what this, is referring. Roundup herbicide may be most important factor in development of Autism and other chronic diseases. How it wrecks human health:

1. Nutritional deficiencies
2. System toxicity
3. Autism
4. Allergies
5. Cardiovascular disease
6. Depression
7. Cancer
8. Infertility
9. Alzheimer's disease
10. Parkinson disease
11. Multiple Sclerosis
12. ALS, and more
13. Obesity
14. Colitis
15. Cohn's disease
16. Bowel disease

* Gastrointestinal disease. Indeed according to Dr Seneff, Glyphosate is possibly the most important factor in the development of multiple chronic diseases and conditions that have become prevalent in Westernized societies, including but not limited to the above mentioned.

How Glyphosate worsens modern Diseases

Research tells us if consumed, it's poison to us! So if we take a further look into this rapidly growing, sprung out-of-control issue that involves not only our health but the health of future generations, then you would see a much sinister story. One report, published in the journal Entropy, argues that Glyphosate residues, around in most commonly consumed foods in Western diet courtesy of GE Sugar, Corn, Soy and Wheat "enhances the damaging effects of other food-borne chemical residues and toxins in the environment to disrupt normal body functions & induce disease."

The claim, Monsanto has steadfastly claimed that Roundup Ready is harmless to animals and humans because the mechanism of action it uses, (which allows it to kill weeds), called the Shikmate pathway, is absent in all animals. However, the Shikmate pathway is present in bacteria, and that's the key to understanding how it causes such widespread systemic harm in both humans and animals. The bacteria in your body outnumber your cells 10 to 1. For every cell in your body, you have 10 microbes of various kinds, and all of them have the Shikmate pathway, so they will ALL respond to the presence of Glyphosate.

Glyphosate causes extreme disruption of the microbe's function and lifecycle. What's worse is, Glyphosate preferentially affects beneficial bacteria, allowing pathogens to overgrow and take over.

At one point, your body has to contend with toxins produced by the pathogens. Once the chronic inflammation sets in, you're well on your way toward chronic and potentially debilitating disease.

In 2009, a French court found Monsanto guilty of lying; falsely advertising it's "environmentally friendly" and claiming it "Left the soil clean." And as "biodegradable."

Monsanto was first established in 1901.

Monsanto's company is publically traded American Multinational agrochemical & Agriculture biotechnology.

Corporation headquartered in Creve Coeur, Greater St. Louis, Missouri. Stock price: 93.74.

Founder: John Francis Queeny.

How does this all tie in you ask? Simply put, we've been lied to. Most people blame bad genetics, not taking in account of all the chemicals, and toxins they are consuming. And this all leads to how it has over time done considerable amount of damage to our DNA, which I will get into as I go along.

Now you are starting to understand that we have been systemically poisoned, no wonder why we have all this crap we have to deal with in our families. Losing people love ones etc. If they only knew as we do then maybe this could have all been prevented? Another one I am going to discuss is

Research Scientist Dr. Anthony Samsel adds" "Monsanto's Trade Secret Studies of Glyphosate show significant incidence of cell tumors of the test and tumorigence growth in multiple organs & tissue. (...) Glyphosate has an inverse dose response relationship and it appears that its effects are highly ph dependent. Both Monsanto and the EPA knew of the deleterious effects of this chemical in 1980 at the conclusion of their multiple long-term assignments. But the EPA hid the results of their findings as "trade secrets." How fucking -

lovely... 2005 quote. If I can pronounce it, it doesn't go in my pie hole! PERIOD!

So in closing: Trade secret law permit corporations to sue anyone who obtains or discloses exclusive proprietary formulas and are used to refuse ingredient disclosure of their products to regulatory agencies. So what good is the EPA and FDA? Monsanto aka Monsatan uses these convenient laws to keep health agencies and independent researchers from testing roundup and other ingredients.

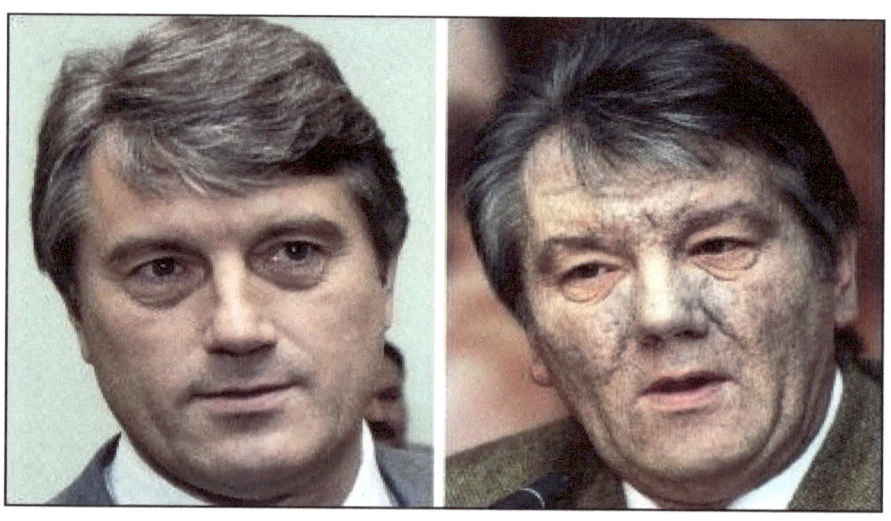

Chloracne – Agent Orange and the after effects.

Agent Orange – better known as Herbicide Orange (HO), is one of its Herbicides warfare program, operation Ranch hand, during the Vietnam War from 1961 to 1971. It was a mixture of equal parts of two Herbicides, 2, 4, 5 – T and 2, 4 –D. It acts on humans by altering the transcription of specific genes. The results aren't pretty.

Dioxin – Research list on cancer. Teterachlorodibenzodioxin or better known as (TCDD). This is known as a human carcinogen.

Dioxin has been found to be an endocrine disrupter; it can cause chloracne, certain cancers, and reproductive and development effects. It is not absorbed by plants nor is it water soluble.

It can attach to the fine soil particles or sediment, which are then carried by water downstream and settle in the bottoms of ponds and lakes. It continues to adversely affect people who eat Dioxin – Contaminated fish, molluscs and fowl produced around point source of Dioxin called "Hotspots". A scale of many decades – and does not degrade readily. The half-life of Dioxin varies depending on where it is found, in humans the half-life is between 11 and 15 years, in surface soil that has been fully exposed to sunlight the half-life is between 1 & 3 years and in the sediment the half-life can be more than 100 years.

If Dioxin permanently alters the intricate internal cellular and chemical balances involved in maintaining good human health, there is serious risk of life-long health problems, which may ultimately lead to mortality.

Food Labeling Act – H.R 15.99 2015

The bill amends the plant Protection Act to allow the sale of a GMO food. (Including imported food and excluding plant pests). Only the F.D.A. has determined through the constitution process that the GMO food is safe and lawful and that determination has been shared with the Department of Agriculture (USDA).

700 million dollar settlement in Alabama PCB lawsuit. And there were 20, 000 won in Anniston and the resident won over PCB contamination.

Michael Taylor – 1976 Attorney. In 2010 – Deputy Commissioner for F.D.A. for foods.

This should not only alarm you but keep you thinking that most of everything we either consume or use is latent with GMO'S. I broke down in simplest terms how it is a hazard to our health, the effects it has on us. This is actually changing our genes. If you mess with any of the RNA/DNA even a small measure of the blueprint in which you were born with, it will break down and create a mutation within the frame. When you do that disease sets in and you're pretty much done for. So are you putting this in your body? Let me put it to you like this, if you are using feminine products, then you are probably doing this without knowing that most feminine hygiene products contain 85% GMO's. Staggering to think about this huh? Ever thought to yourself, um, no... I can't believe this! But if you think about it in this way, that GMO cotton makes up 93% of the US cotton supply. (2010).

GMO soybeans make up 93-95% of the US. (2010).

I'm going to now take it a step forward. Yikes you say what more can she possible have to offer or bring to the table? Oh, I have plenty more.

If this is all happen to us undetected, then when do we wake up and fight back? If you're sick, and always feeling like one foot is in the grave how are you to fight anyhow? As you can see this is a silent killer, a slow poisoning if you will. So if they are gene splicing, and putting all kind of DNA, bacteria and other organisms that are causing harm to us, what else is there left to do? A lot more... If you can conceive it, then it's probably already been patented or tested out on humans in trails. Are you a genie pig? Do you feel like a lab rat now? This is nothing really new, it's just careful hid so no one ever questions what is going on behind the curtain. One only has to start to become inquisitive and be a bit more introspective about this all in order to further understand it on the level in which it is presented. Is anything really organic anymore? Do you even know what PLU codes to look for as you're browsing through the produce section? No, I can tell you because there is not much labeling going on. Ever heard of Prop 37? Probably not, it's for labeling GMO's and this allows the consumer to know what they are actually putting into their body, which is their vessel. Don't you like all of us have a right to know?

Glyphosate

on farmland

(only one year and only one pesticide...it all adds up.)

Estimated Agricultural Use for Glyphosate , 2013 (Preliminary)

EPest-Low

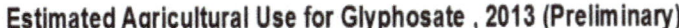

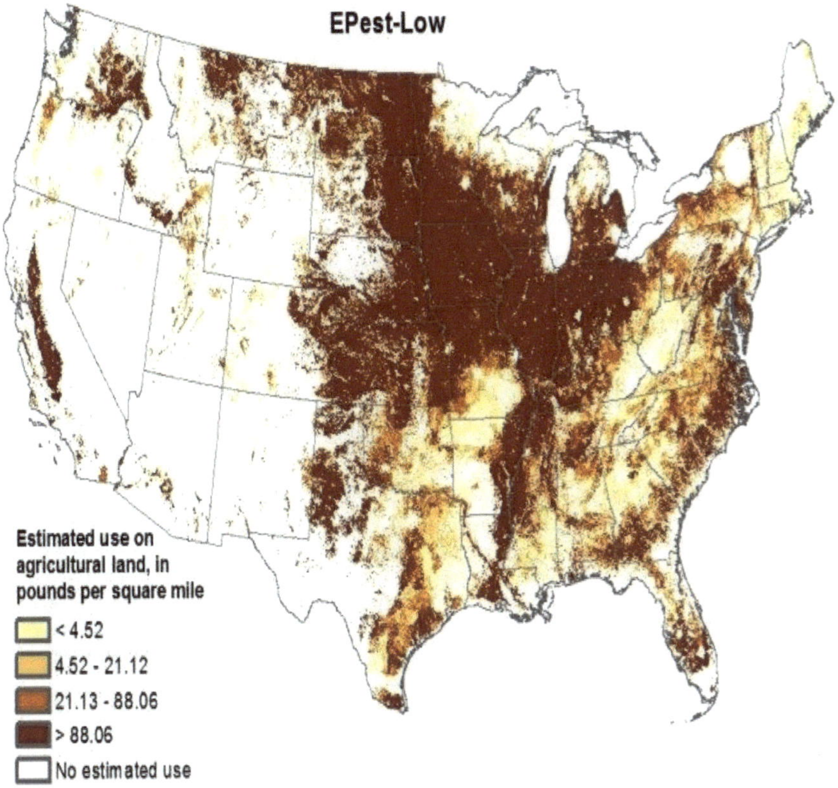

Source: http://water.usgs.gov/nawqa/pnsp/usage/maps/show_map.php?year=2013&map=24D&hilo=L&disp=2%2C4-D

10 NON-GMO NEWS STORIES YOU DON'T WANT TO MISS!

1. U.S. farmers lost millions when key trading partners decided to restrict wheat imports after a rogue form of genetically engineered wheat, not approved by the USDA nor sold commercially, was discovered in Oregon.
2. A new peer-reviewed long-term feeding study found that pigs fed a combination of GMO soy and corn suffered more frequent severe stomach inflammation and enlargement of the uterus.
3. 4,600 stores nationwide including large chains like Whole Foods and Target have said no to genetically engineered salmon.
4. Big victory in the Supreme Court: Human genes can no longer be patented!
5. 26 states such as Connecticut, Vermont, Maine, and Washington, along with members of Congress, are acting to ensure consumers have a right to know about GMOs.
6. Chipotle announces they will source non-GMO ingredients and label current GMOs in their restaurant chain.
7. A new peer-reviewed study showed that low level exposure to glyphosate causes estrogen-sensitive breast cancer cells to grow.
8. A groundbreaking new study revealed that 44% of EU city dwellers, from 18 countries, are contaminated with Monsanto's product Roundup.
9. Target announces new non-GMO line of food products to be sold at all of their stores.
10. U.S. approves a label for meat and liquid egg products that includes a claim about the absence of GMOs. These newly labeled products can only come from animals that never ate feed containing GMO ingredients like corn, soy, cotton and alfalfa.

GMOiNSiDE
Coalition Powered by Green America

GMO Foods

For more information go to **olmag.co/gmo-foods**

Tomato

Tomatoes have been genetically modified, but they are not being grown commerically at this time

Rice

GMO rice has been approved but is not yet being used commercially

Sweet Corn

More than 70 percent of corn grown in the United States has been genetically engineered

Summer Squash

Farmers don't like GMO squash but some experts say GM squash have blended with wild squash

Salmon

GMO salmon has not been approved by the FDA, but it will be very soon

Canola Oil

87% of canola grown commercially, and 80% of wild caniola is GMO

Yeast

GMO yeast for wine has been approved

Alfalfa
GMO alfalfa is contaminating non GMO alfalfa crops at a rapid rate

Wheat
Unapproved GMO has contaminated wheat fields, and we don't yet know the extent of it

Sugar Beets
90% of Sugar Beets (used to make 50% of our sugar) are GMO

Soy
More than 93% of soybeans the United States produces are genetically modified

Peas
Peas have been genetically modified but are not approved or availabile

Hawaiian Papaya

Most Hawaiian papaya is GMO, even many organic crops are contaminated

Cotton

At least half of cotton grown in the world is GMO

organic lifestyle MAGAZINE

Point I am trying to make here is that they want you sick, to remain ill. They can't make money off you if you are a healthy person. They can't fill their pockets until something happens when you have to do that. My entirely family has solely relied on the very drug industry that has destroyed their lives, health and overall lifestyle. They were sure they were in capable hands at the time of their check up. It's sad to know that they never sought after an alternative method. I watched them all go downhill very fast. It was horrible, for each of them meant a lot to me. I think over the years I just accepted that it was going to be that way no matter how hard I tried to help them or show them a different path in life; they just shut me out and ignored all of it. This made me feel like why I even bother trying to help them when they never truly wanted to help themselves. It was hard watching it though, I will be honest. And I knew things they didn't because I took the time to learn it and study to the point I had lost sleep and it affected my health too. I guess I was trying to be the savior, and it really boils down to what you're willing to sacrifice in the end. Being called crazy because I was more aware and awake wasn't ever easy. That didn't stop me though; I kept it going and look where it has led me, down a damn rabbit hole, which is where! Hence my 4th book title.

It all comes to us being lied to, time and again. It takes a lot of heart to keep going through this all. I won't let to you think I can sit here and pretend it has been a bed of roses, it hasn't! I have however, just kept believing that my heart could somehow change the way things have turned out. We have been lied to, and put into an illusion. A state of unreal consciousness. Babylon means Confusion, spiritual confusion that is, which is Hebrew. That is what is what we are in now. We live in the land of confusion. Do I have your attention now? Are you connecting the dots? Does it disturb you to know this kind of information? None of us were taught to go within ourselves when we wanted to learn something or solve a problem, yet that's where the greatest wisdom lies based on the presumption that the knowledge exists outside of you. But it is your decision made from the zenith of your magnificent awareness and divine brilliance. You are divine, I am divine. You are a being of unlimited awareness and extraordinary potential! But how could you even possibly know this unless you had some type of mentor or divine intervention? So I want you to keep in mind the starting point of all creation and certainly with any change we wish to manifest is with the desire end result in mind. Let me leave you on this note. God's people are destroyed for lack of knowledge.

Let me purpose to say that if we were more aware of these events' red flags or just plain fooling us by the grand illusion. But if you were to discover this for yourself would you not want to dig deeper to discover the truth? Life for instance they make us sterile by the food we consume. (Epicyte) is the silent sterilization process. Part of the depopulation agenda. Wouldn't you want to be consciously aware of this happening? Would you not try to avoid the very food that does this to you and your family? I think we all have the right to know, don't you? We all have the right to Life, Liberty and the pursuit of happiness! Why is it we are so quick to point the finger at bad genetics? Why do we always look to just temporarily fix the bullet hole? Why do we think we can just but an average size bandage on it to rid the problem? We have to look deeper than that for the answers. I think you have to be really hungry for it to actually accept it for what it truly is, and hey... maybe that is how we can change things. There by helping others by informing them in which they aren't currently aware of. It takes courage and strength to stay on the course.

The laws put in place to protect us are being ignored. And what's worse is that those laws are about to be superseded, if the powers that be have their way. United Nations Commission is a joint intergovernmental body of the Food & Agriculture Organization of the United Nations FAO & WHO.

Food Code is a set of regulations that aim to outlaw only health information in the connection with the vitamins and limited free access to natural therapies on a worldwide scale. Instead of focus on Food Safety, codex is using its power to promote worldwide restrictions on vitamins and food supplements, severely limiting their ability and dosages. The actual goal is to outlaw health products and information on vitamins and dietary supplements, except those under their control. These regulations would supersede United States Domestic Laws without the American People's voice or vote in the matter. Food control equals people control – population control. GATT, World Trade Organization, the United States agreed to HARMONIZE its domestic laws to be the international standards. The Uruguay Round Agreement. The United States, Canada, the European, Japan, most of Asia, and South America. These are already signed up with the International Standards.

Money & Profits at the expense of the people

Established under heavy influence of the pharmaceutical industry in 1963 following resolutions passed at the Eleventh session of the conference of Food & Agriculture Organization of the United Nations in 1961, and at the Sixteenth World Health Assembly in 1963.

Corporate Globalization and the erosion of democracy

WHO – World Health Organization was formed in 1994 harmonizing Food Standards globally for easy trade between countries. So I like to elaborate on some of the things that are allowed into our food that we consume. This thing I am going to discuss is called POPS, which is Persistent Organic Pollutants. There was once the dirty dozen, and now it's down to 7 but before that there were 9, they were pesticides. That leaves us with 3,275 different pesticides that are presently going into our bodies! What do think it's doing to your vessel? God's heavenly vessel?

Changing it, that is what...I will assure you that if you happen to be curious and look on the site of Codex Alimentarius, you will then see that there are well over 200 pesticides that are in our produce, meats, dairy etc...

These are compounds that are resistant to environmental degradation through chemical, biological and photolytic processes. Biomagnifications – even small releases of POPS can have significant impacts. Conventional crops have 4 times more pesticides residue than organic crops.

The lists of the pesticides I provide below will help you better understand that what we are dealing with is mass genocide, in other words calculated, and well orchestrated murder. It is a slow poisoning, and it will gradually work its way in and break down the very system you need to work probably in order to heal and repair. Without the organs functioning and working properly, you die! See the connection? See that we've all bought into a corporate lie? The medical conspiracy of all time is making you believe you can't heal without medical intervention. Codex Alimentarius is Latin for Code. Some of the food additives are as follows:

1. Aspartame – Found in most diet sodas, gums.
2. BHA – Found in cereal, butter, beer and more.
3. BHT – Food and care products
4. Potassium bromated – Food additive - Breads.
5. Tartrazine - Cereals, desserts, snack food, shampoos and even cosmetics all contain this harmful colorant.

You might ask why I am discussing all these things here today, in this book. What we don't know can hurt us, and our love ones. I don't believe in ignorance is bliss anymore. This goes much deeper than that. It's about being aware of the world in which we live in, and what is going on in it. I use to think I was a bit out there because I had this kind of knowledge, but I thought wait a minute, why have it all if I can't do anything with it? I think that is when God showed me what I was sent here for, my purpose. To teach, to inform, to grow and yes, to evolve. That is our birthright, though it has been taken from us and we didn't even realize it. I think it really all boils down to who you are as person. Actions speak, words are cheap. My action today shows the kind of person I am. So, this might be my final chapter. But I wanted to be something I could be proud of, and never gave up on. This was my dream... That is why I am sharing it along with my art. Deep down inside I know we all can make a difference. We're powerful beyond even our own conscious understanding. I use to think because I was a woman; I was just that, put into a box and labeled, I have woken from that slumber and know otherwise different than that now. I stepped into the light a long time ago. So, what you are reading today is years of compiling hours upon hours of research and dedication to getting it done. Hopefully out there in the right hands. To the people that deserve to have this kind of knowledge. To basically understand what took place while we were here. Maybe to shed a different kind of light, but light nonetheless. And what I am talking about is how we have been systematically dumb down, put into a different vibration, by the way of energy, and how it can be screwed with if not given the key elements to keep it functioning and working properly. What I am trying to get across to you and this world is that we can't rise up if we don't know what we are facing here! Plain and simple as that. There is nothing more to it. It all starts with us and it will finish that way. Though many have eyes to see and ears to hear, they ignore it all. In the world of the blind, the one eye man is king! Spiritual knowledge is one of the highest to obtain, because that is what we are, spirits in the material world. And our hearts will go on.

I wanted to share this picture with you because it is the light that is in all of us. Do you ever just lie down and see a light ever so present as this? It's the spiritual eye, the 3rd eye. I do when I close my eyes I see this ray of light shooting out from my all seeing eye. So this is our connection to the divine, what has been swiped from under us. How to get it back takes time and a lot of meditation. It takes practice to stay in the place, that sacred place. Let no man, or anyone for that matter disturb your peace of mind!

It's a freeing feeling when you get it all out. It's even more freeing when you can feel good about sharing what took you so long to understand. And the light will keep you safe for all your days here. I do wish I could have gone back and corrected all the mistakes, all the pitfalls, or just the people that have since then all passed to the other side.

You can see yourself as a drop or a drop in an ocean. And even that one drop ripples out and affects all that it surrounds. That is how powerful we are! In a sea of consciousness, we are that ripple sent out throughout space & time. And only love can transcend it all! One heart can change it.

Peacock ore, very magnetic looking huh? Mined in Mexico, and known for its iridescent colors. I find that stones have healing properties. And can alter or affect your mood, just as music or colors, art does. **Bornite, also known as peacock ore, is a sulfide mineral with chemical composition Cu_5FeS_4 that crystallizes in the orthorhombic system (pseudo-cubic).**

I choose this picture to show you that there are missing pieces, but inside is where you will always find the answers. Let no one tell you those answers, God all talks to us in different ways, in which different information is given. That piece that is missing is the key to your happiness! That missing piece will come to you when you least expect it. Search your soul and find your truth, let no one tell you what that truth is. That is between you and the creator! Let's heal, no harm, let's come together not fight in arms. Let's make it a better place for generations to come.

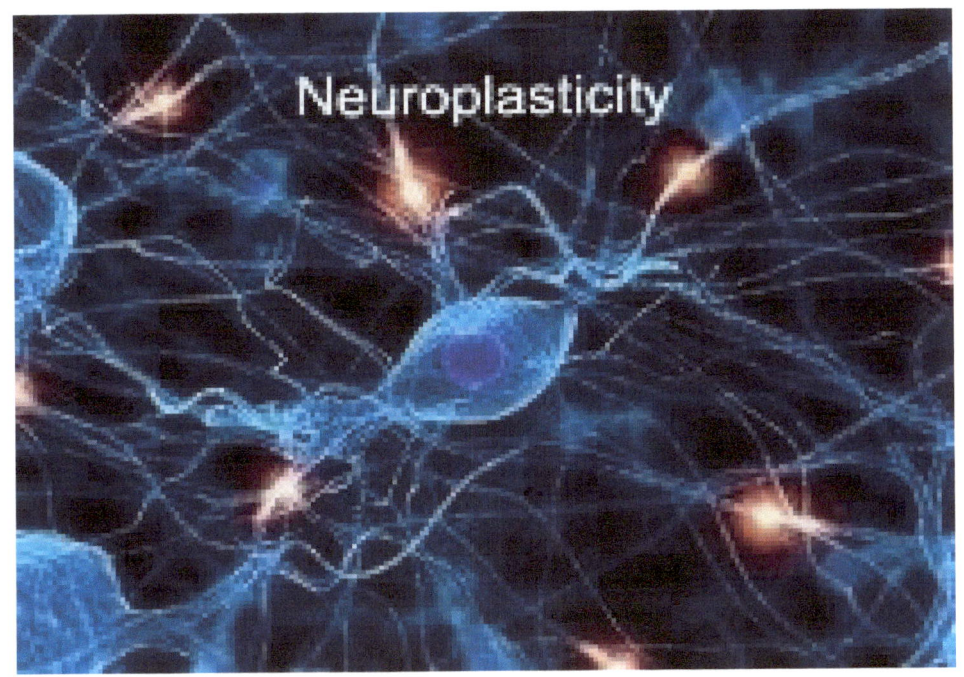

Your cerebral cortex is a mysterious thing, it can rewire its connections and use those to have a different way to solve or think about a problem. It's an amazing tool to have. If you sharpen it, well, it gets better. The more you use it, the better it becomes.

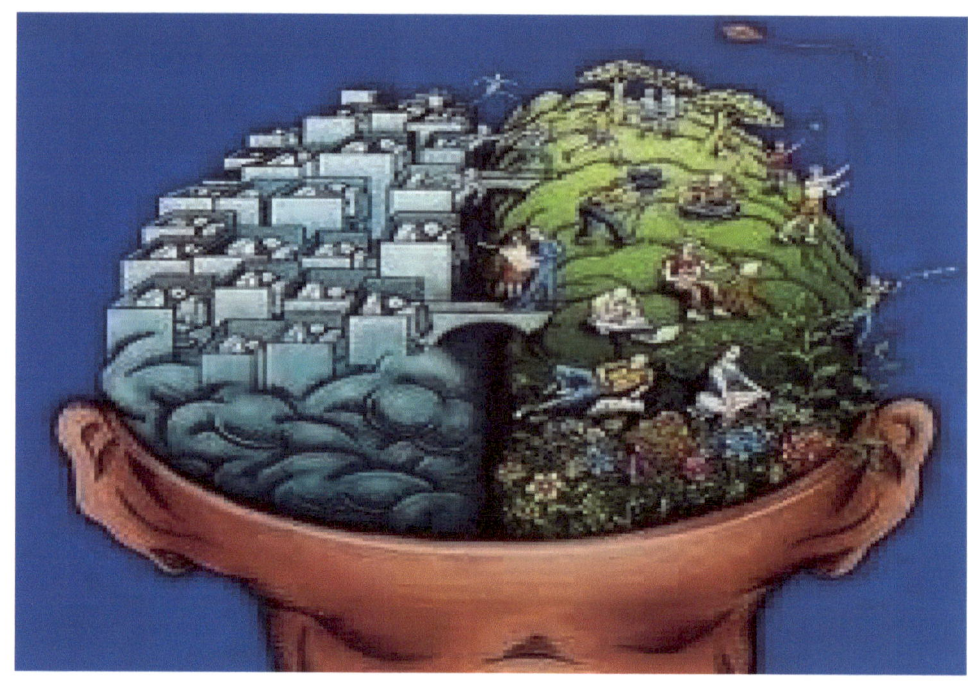

The right side, which is the spiritual side. The left side, which is the logical side. So the question comes in the form of how do we bridge them? When is there a time when they work together, **I FEEL** too much, **I THINK** too much. When can there ever be a balance? It comes in the form of peace through not trying to fight them. To accept that you feel, that you think, you think the minute you are able to process information, the minute you have to come into this world. We are continually doing that no matter what. You can't switch it off. So what are thoughts? If we are made in the image of God, is it not fair to stay that thoughts are **LIGHT**, and that makes us Light beings. We need the sun, just as the flowers and grass need it to grow (Photosynthesis), getting that energy we need to grow and be healthy, and turning that sun light into energy for us. Why do you think we are called children of the sun for?

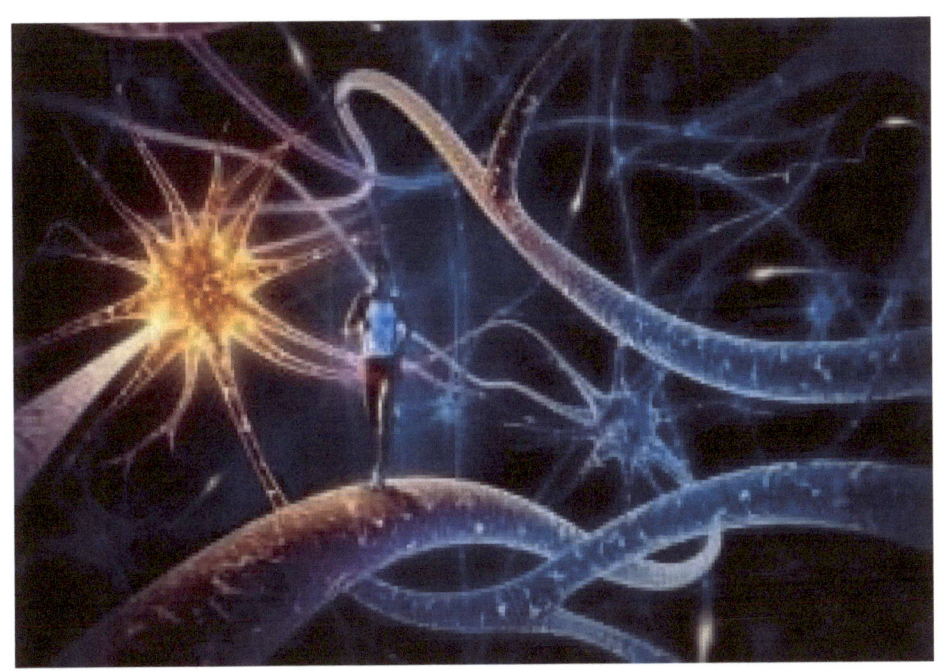

Does it always feel like you are running somewhere? Does it always feel like the more you are running the further you get away from what it really is that you desire? We're all running to get to a certain place in life. What is that place? Is it the finish line? Even if you finish last, you still finish!

Maybe it's a race against time....

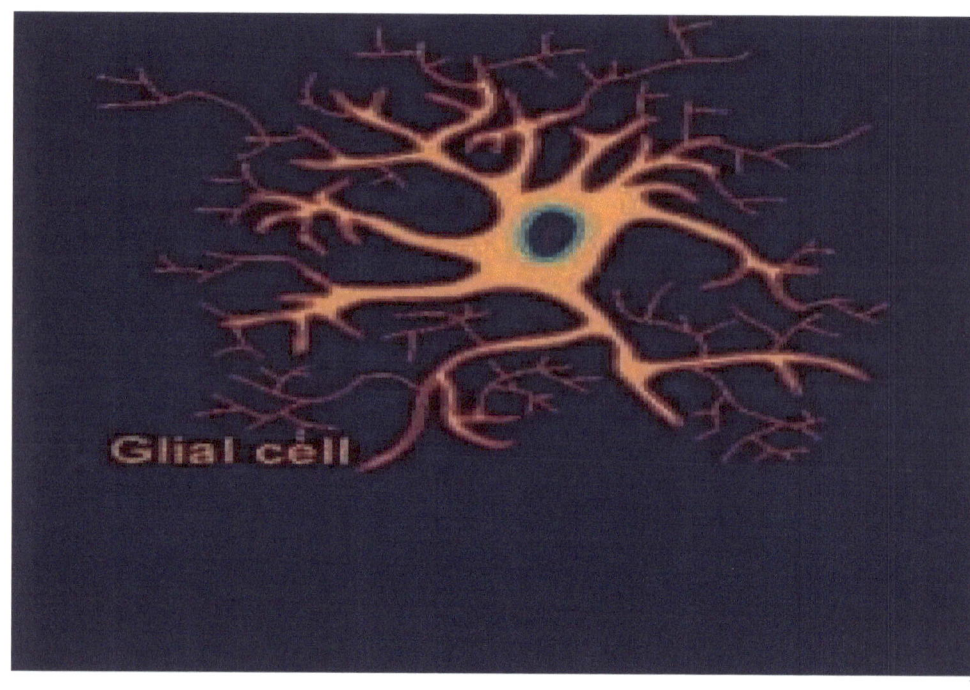

Glial cells – Greek for glue. Sulci – unusual patterns, grooves. As intelligence increases, so does the level of Glial cells to the ratio of neuron, a copious supply. Astrocyte – A star-shaped Glial cell of the central nervous system. Creative genius minds, usually love the Arts and Science, and prefer to be self taught. When Einstein's brain was examined they found the he more Glial cells, which are known for giving him is brilliance. Meaning that this was responsible for his ability to think differently from the rest of us, the ability to imagine being a beam of light riding it like a wave. He had a unique way of processing information. He, I THINK, is one of the greatest minds besides Nikola Tesla, which is another one that has blown me away. Tesla had 700 patents under us belt, and the Death Ray being one of them. Calling all Free Thinkers! He was better known for his Alternate Current. Light, of course he didn't invent it, but he surely was able to find a way it can be harnessed and the way it was distributed. The one invention they tried to suppress was the Tesla Coils. The concept that Earth itself is a magnet that can generate electricity (electromagnetism) utilizing frequencies as a transmitter. All that was needed on the other end was a receiver – much like a radio. X-rays was another one he invented. The radio, Tesla invented the radio years before Marconi. This radio only needed a transmitter and receiver, which was demonstrated in 1893 during a presentation before the National Electric Light Association. In 1897 Tesla applied for two patents US 645576, and US 649621. Remote Control – Patent No. 613809, the first remote controlled model boat, demonstrated in 1898. Utilizing several large batteries; radio signals controlled switches, which then energized the boats propeller, rudder, and scaled-down running lights. Radio controlled tanks were introduced by the Germans in WWII and developments in this realm have since slid quickly away from the direction of human freedom. The Electric Motor – Finally popularized by Car brandishing his name. Suffice to say that Tesla's invention of a motor with rotating magnetic fields could have free mankind much sooner from the strongholds of the Elite, oops, I mean Big Oil. Nevertheless, this invention has fundamentally changed the landscape of what we now take for granted: industrial fans, household appliances, water pumps, machine tools, power tools, disk drives, electric wristwatches and compressors. Robotics, yes... The idea that led him to believe that all living beings driven by external impulses. Laser, which would be the Death ray, I mentioned above. But lasers have benefited us in our surgically applications in a very transformative way. Wireless Communication and free energy. Tesla built a tower that could, and was backed up by J.P Morgan. That could transmit and collect data by the use of Natural Frequencies by the way of our Universe. This included a wide range of data, and information through images, voice messages, and text. This represented the first wireless communications, but it could also be said that this was free energy that could utilize to form a world-wide web connecting all people to harness the free energy around them. This never sat too well with J.P Morgan, this mean free energy with virtually no charge! The research that harnessed electricity from the ionosphere at a facility was called Wardeclyffe – this was a necessary step toward freedom information. Aren't you tired of not having a higher level of Education?

Perhaps the one they never wanted us to have in the first place. Are you ready to discover what the universe has in store for us? More importantly use it and what it has to offer to all of us!

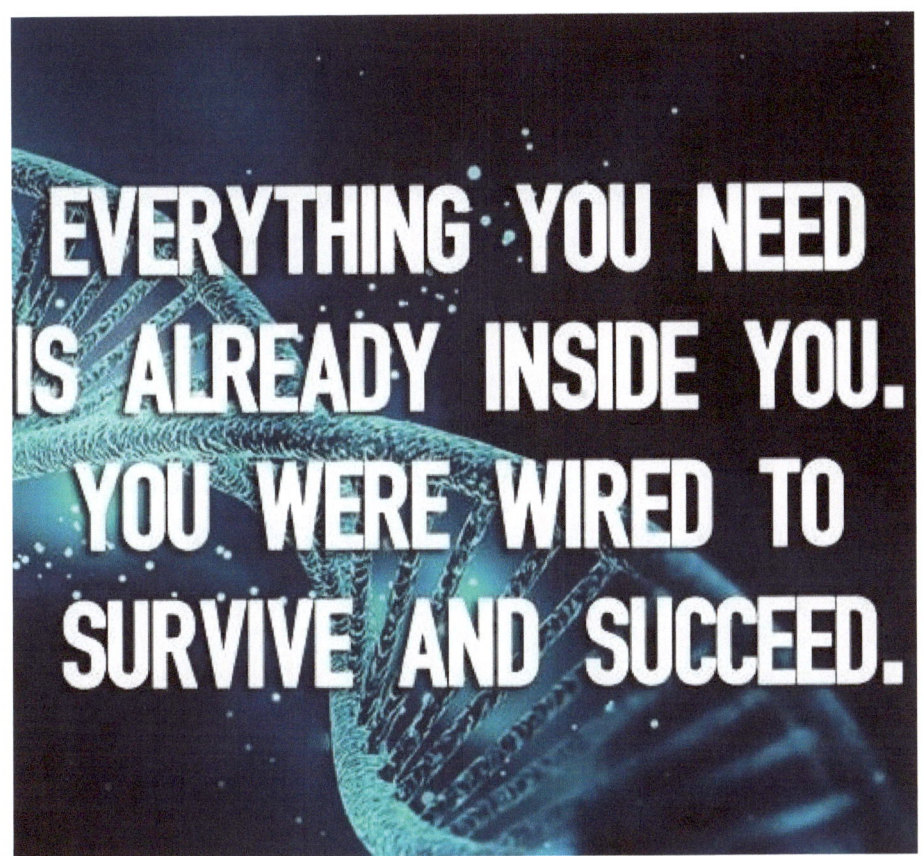

The Mind is God. And we are Gods and Goddesses! And if we know this coming here don't you think our lives would have been much different. Knowing we are divine and we too can reach divinity through enlightenment. That part is through the heart, through your spirit communication to the divine.

Ok, I am going to go a step further. You now are aware of free energy, frequencies, and human behavior, intent etc. But what if all you ever knew was just to keep you busy, controlled and in a slave mentality? Never question things, never think outside the box. Go outside! No box required. Don't you at the end of the day, a long day, think to yourself, this overwhelming feeling that you belong and are connected to everything? Everything you want to have access to, that is. What if I told you that we are all mini creators, yes, we are the co-creators of our realities and the universe we know serves us. Are purposes is to keep going till the end of the tunnel, even if you finish last, you still finish! The universe tells us, that despite any kind of setbacks or headaches, that we are strong enough to get through all the challenges or hard balls the universe or the world, people throw at us!

You hold the flames, the external, and the internal. How bright do you want yours to burn? You can achieve balance through much practice. But to live life like this takes a lot of patients. Don't attempt to do it if you think you don't have time for it or the patients it requires to reach this level of consciousness. That takes much soul searching.

The rainbow, which stands for the chakras of the body, the energy centers. You are a rainbow too! Where are all my rainbow warriors at?

The violet flame – to channel this you must visualize you putting a protective shield over the earth incased in a light purple one. This can be done by believing you have that kind of power. What do you think prayer is? It's a torsion wave that you are generating and being sent out into the universe. Hopefully to be answered from the creator/God.

You hold this world in your hands; you alone have always had that power. Power is knowledge, and knowledge is all about how you use it. Take a look inside your heart!

You are responsible for the kind of energy you send out into this world. What kind of energy are you sending out?

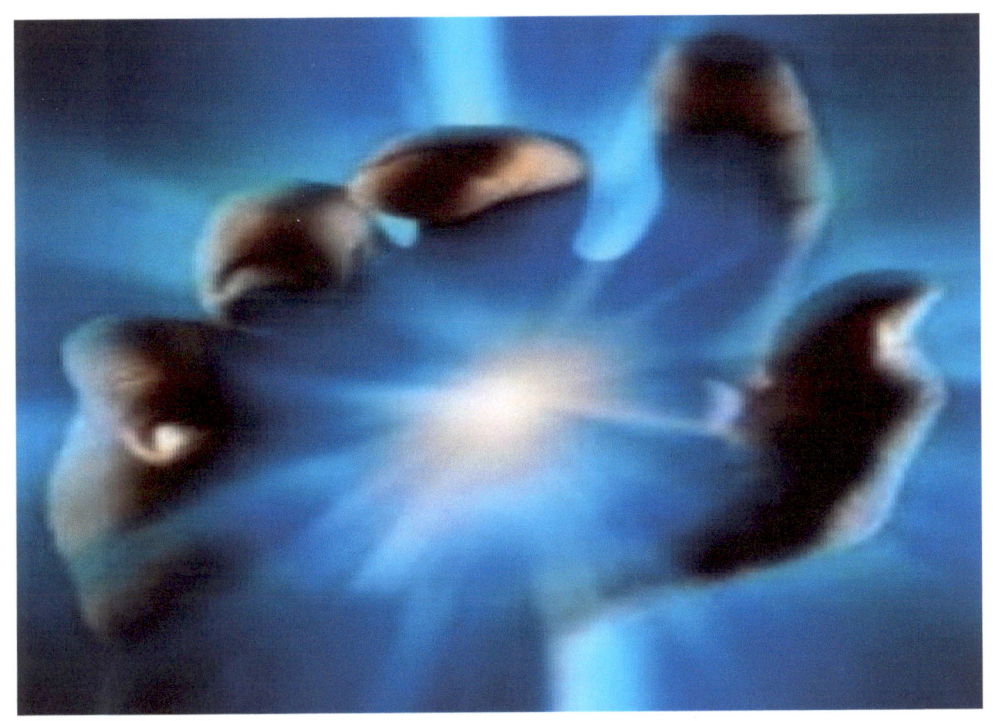

A healing hand? The power to heal is inside us all. A touch can be, but are we really touching anything? It's merely just atoms that are bouncing off another atom. So are we truly touching, no.. We are just letting them feel our kinetic energy.

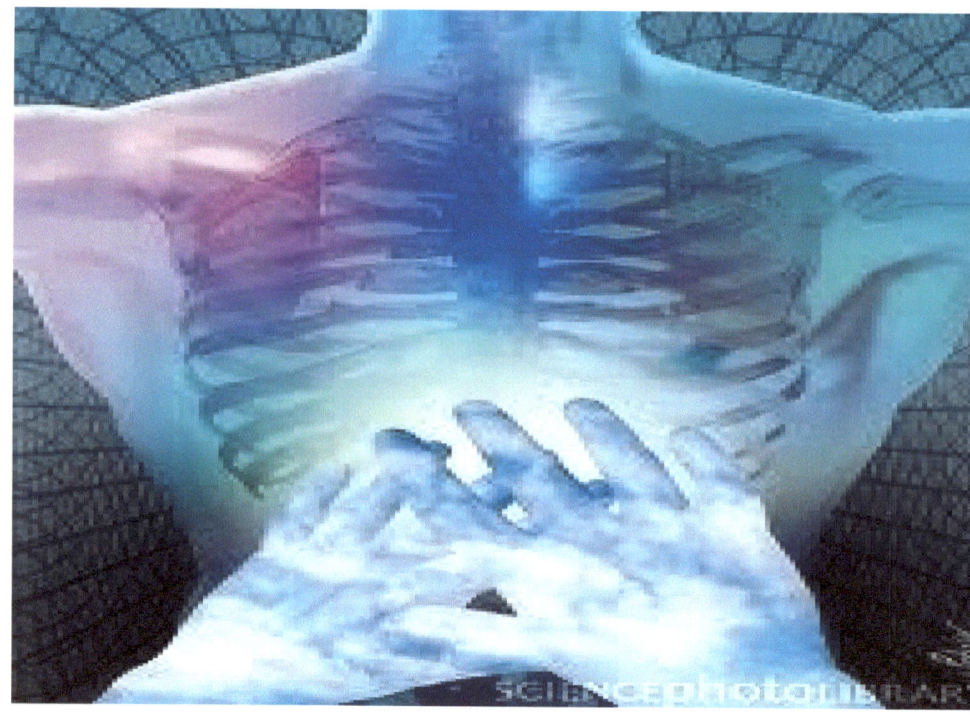

This image is to show you from up above how it would look if you were to witness this energy being emitted by your own two sets of eyes. And focus is all it takes. There are all forms and sorts of energy. One is what kind of energy are you focusing on? Destroying or healing? Are you looking to destroy an empire or build one? Same goes for bodies, you can repair it or damage it further. The choice is yours in the end.

Find your truth, and even if that means starting over again in life. Sometimes life has to shake us back awake, so we can live out what we're meant for. If no one else believes in you, you believe in you! Hold on to that dream, that goal, the end result! Whatever it is that you define as your happy place, happy thought or whatever brings you enjoyment. Don't let them jade you, don't let them take your shine!

The sun sets and rises another day. You need this to live here on Earth. You need love to know your name!

When we lose someone we love at a young age, unexpectedly, there is most certainly a reason. Their death is not without good cause, it is because their fate is to be spiritual guide for someone here in the physical world. To us they die young, however theirs is not really a death, it is just their time here in the physical world and they're done, it's their time to return home. They are never forgotten. Death is but a door, time is but a window. And even though processing all this at a young age, I was able to comprehend some of it, not all. And it's never easy losing someone who you love. Love to know our name. Why is it that it seems the one thing that is the hardest to obtain, say and show? What if we never found love? They say the greatest love is inside of you! I suggest you find it.

So, let me purpose that we are all quantum energy, all vibrating at different energy levels. Remember energy cannot be created nor can it be destroyed, it only transforms into something entirely different from its current form it is. Most wonder how the universe was made, and that brings me to this, do you believe in the existence of multi-verses?

What about the primordial gravitational waves – ripples in space-time created just after the universe began? If evidence proves right, then it would provide that space – time expanded at many times the speed of light just after the Big Bang 13.8 billion years ago. So that means each universe within the multi-verse can have a different set of constants and physical laws. Quantum Fluctuations of the inflation field. Chaotic inflation theory model quantum fluctuations in the rate of inflations. These regions with a higher rate of inflation to end the other regions. This allows inflation to continue forever, to produce future – eternal flation. The energy scale is around 10^16 billion electrons volts, or roughly 1 trillion times greater than the levels achieved by Earth's most powerful particle accelerator, the LHC. Large Hadron Collider – this is in Switzerland, it's known as Cern – And they are hoping to find the God particle, the one that is responsible for the creation of everything. They did however discover the Higgs Boson. They theories of it being switched on, thus allowing for Pandora's Box to be open. The head Scientist even said that if we open it we are not sure of what is to come out of the portal, dimensional opening. Nor do they know how to close it? Scary? Why yes… it really is when you look at the facts. I have read my Bible – Basic instructions before leaving Earth. (LAUGHTER).

The book clearly indicates we were given the key to the bottomless pit! Why do they have a Cern Key then? Makes you think huh. So are we playing with fire here? Are we messing with something that should be left alone? Who benefits from this? Let's say they are successful, they open the gate, think in terms of a Stargate/Project Pegasus. Yes, there have been many covert projects from our lovely government. (Sarcasm smirk). What are they not telling us? Obliviously they have left out quite a lot and hidden a great deal from us! So let's recap – We live in world run by psychotic individuals who for no other reason don't want us to ever reach our highest potential. Why you ask? Because when we become enlighten, we are able to see through all the lies. We can stop, retract and start a revolution of change. Yes, that is what we are. This information only serves us if we are consciously seeking it out. Ok, we cover the crazy ones that are controlling us through education, the food we consume, the money they make called Fiat money. And let's not forget we all need food to stay healthy and alive, vibrant, and focused. We all need a job in order the live, and have a roof over our heads. But what if we have been silenced? Why is it we never speak of things that truly matter? Don't you believe you do matter, if not why do you feel you don't?

It's about power here, those who have it and those who don't have it. Would you even know how to use it if you knew you had this to begin with? Maybe it's high time you took it back. Speak up; let your voice be heard! By whatever means is necessary. And if it doesn't serve your highest good, then let it go.

Our planet is in a state of transition; therefore, while we appear to be undergoing traumatic upheaval, the frequency of the entire planet is actually rising/16.5. This challenges and pushes to the surface whatever does not resonate with the new frequencies, making all that is destructive, disorient, and by bringing in more the energy that is in alignment. We have the healing ability on all levels, the physical, mental, emotional and spiritual, to assist other beings at this time both facilitating the release of energies that are not aligned with new higher frequencies. The more disruptive, the more visible. So now that you are starting to understand more as we continue along, then you will see where I am about to take this. It all comes down to HEALTH & keeping your energies pure. How do we go about this you might ask? If we are energy, then we too need clean energy to keep things healing, repairing. How do we go about this? First you have to know the driving power of your cells, all cells need oxygen, and all cells need clean energy in order to work like they are supposed to. If our food is being tainted and so is our air and the soil, then how are we to actually get our hands on the good stuff? Well, I say if you really want to know what is going in your body, grow your own food – Heirloom seeds, they are harder to come by nowadays. The driving power behind all of it is your Mitochondria cell. So let's say that your 3rd eye is covered and your mitochondria are breaking down at a faster rate than what it was intended to. I just broke down the disrupters, the ones responsible for this. The energy source for cellular activity: Cytochrome molecules are believed to be responsible for light absorption in mitochondria, the energy source for cellular activity. And it is believed that LED light absorption causes conformational changes in the antenna molecules with the mitochondrial membrane. Proton translocation initiates a pump, which ultimately leads to energy for conversion of ADP to ATP. This essentially recharges the "cell battery" and provides more energy. The whole point is to create mitochondria (fresh). Without mitochondria integrity, malfunction/mutation of the cell begins, creating a number of age related issues. Keep in mind that frequencies also play a key role in DNA & mitochondria repair. Thus stimulating new mitochondria growth & protection from the cell degenerative melt down process.

Stimulating cell growth by electromagnetic fields/sounds.

How can this be done you ask? Well it's simple really. You have frequencies that break down your body as well as repair it. So if you have a higher frequency, let's say 528 hertz or higher than that is DNA repair. Anything below that number won't do very much for your cells. Now PQQ preserves the mitochondria cell, and creates new ones. Resveratrol – is required to active the AMPK gene – thus SIRT1 is turned on! Clinical studies prove beyond a shadow of doubt that mice live up to 20 to 30 years longer than expected when given a certain dose. Lifespan increases, cognitive abilities return, muscles and tissue regenerate. 20 mg is needed this being equivalent to 41 glasses of red wine. Blueberries also have this in them. Glycine – there are two genes that are active in turning back the clock of time. These genes are none other than the (GAT & SHMT2). This is one of the 27 amino acids.

Amino acids break-down:

1. Resveratrol   5. Cysine   9. Aspartic acid
2. Glycine   6. Tetrapeptide 10. MercaptA1

3. Inner salts   7. Nucleic acid   11. Alkane acid
4. PQQ   8. Nucleotides   12. Octane Acid

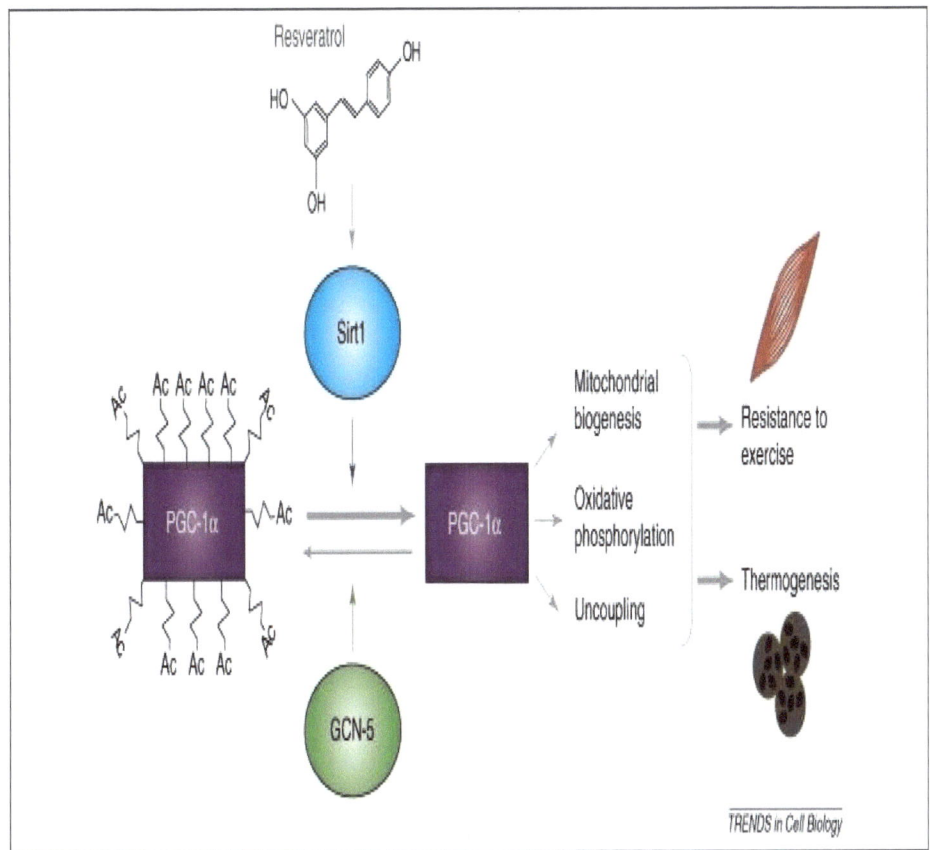

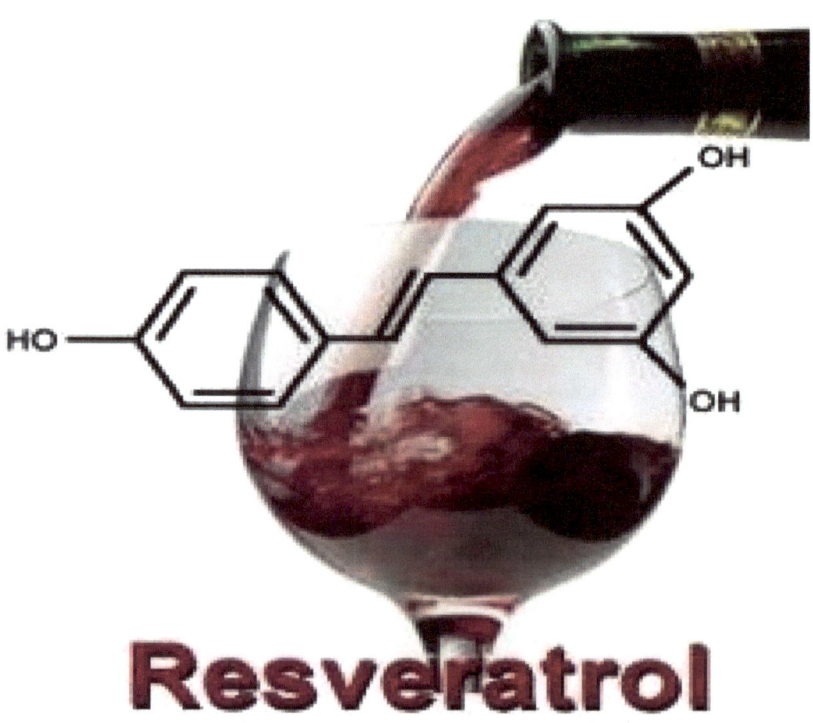

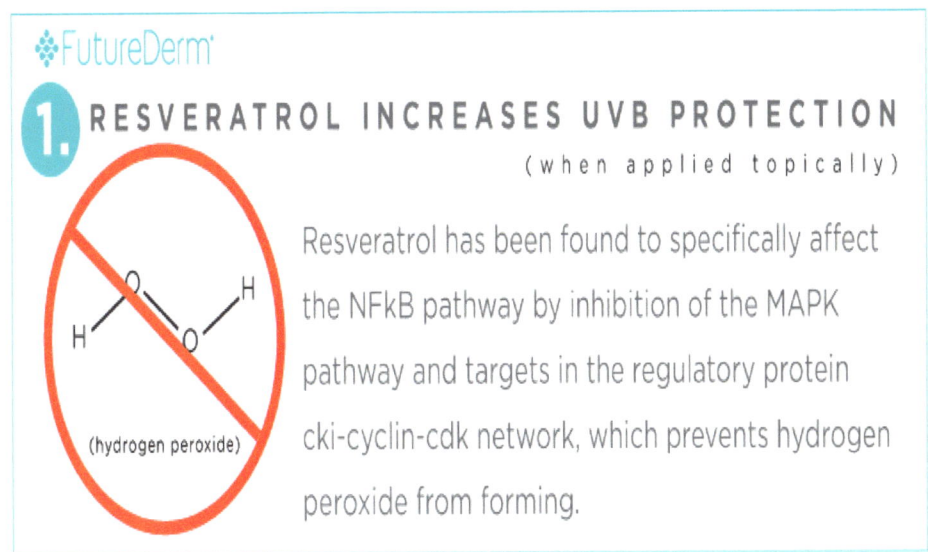

Amino acids, protein and the building blocks for optimal performance. Zwitterions, a hybrid, di polar having half one positive ion (the cation) and on the other end, a negative (ion). Perhaps the best things beside the essential amino acids are cell salts: 12 essential minerals for optimal cellular health:

1. Potassium Phosphate
2. Sodium Sulphate
3. Potassium chloride
4. Calcium Fluoride
5. Magnesium Phosphate
6. Sodium Phosphate
7. Calcium Sulphate
8. Silica
9. Calcium Phosphate
10. Sodium Chloride
11. Ferrous Phosphate
12. Potassium sulphate

pH Food Chart

DRINK IONIZED WATER
1 LITER per 30 lbs
DAILY

⇑

Consume Freely

Alkaline pH

Most foods get more acidic when cooked

⇓

Neutral pH

⇑

20:1
It takes 20 parts of ALKALINITY to Neutralize 1 part ACIDITY in the body

Acidic pH

⇓

Consume Sparingly or never

⇓

pH 10.0 — 1,000x more Alkaline — High Alkaline Ionized Water

Raw Spinach	Red Cabbage	Dandelion	Alfalfa Grass
Raw Broccoli	Raw Celery	Seaweeds	Barley Grass
Artichokes	Cauliflower	Raw Onions	Wheat Grass
Raw Asparagus	Collard Greens	Lemons & Limes	Black Radish
	Cucumber	Rhubarb Stalks	Soy Sprouts
	Raw Kale	Soy Lecithin-pure	Chia Sprouts

pH 9.0 — 100x more Alkaline

Avocados	Red Radish	Raw Peas	Garlic or Chives
Borage Oil	Red Beets	Raw Eggplant	Dog/Shave Grass
Green Tea	Raw Tomato	Alfalfa Sprouts	Straw Grass
Most Lettuce	French Beans	Green Beans	Lemon Grass
Raw Zucchini	Parsley-Cilantro	Beet Greens	Cayenne Pepper

pH 8.0 — 10x more Alkaline

Brussel Sprouts	Lima Beans	Raw Almonds	Chicory
Endive	Soy Beans-Fresh	Wild Rice	Olives
Green Cabbage	Navy Beans	Quinoa	Bell Peppers
Cooked Spinach	Cooked Peas	Millet	Watercress
Cooked Broccoli	Cook Eggplant	Flax Seed Oil	White Radish
Cook Asparagus	Sour Grapefruit	Coconut Water	Lamb's Lettuce

pH 7.0 — Most Tap Water

Municipalities adjust tap water to be +/- 7.3 by using Chlorine to keep pH high enough to eliminate any bacterial growth etc.

HUMAN BLOOD pH is 7.365

Most Olive Oils	Fennel Seeds	
Pumpkin Seeds	Sunflower Seeds	
Primrose Oil	Leeks (bulbs)	
Marine Lipids	Coconut & Oil	
Sesame Seeds	Barley	
Raw Goat Milk	Sprouted Breads	

pH 6.0 — 10x more Acidic

Fresh H₂O Fish	Macadamias	Watermelon	Dates
Lentils	Grapes	Cantaloupe	Peaches
Spelt	Hazelnuts	Cherries	Oranges
Soy Flour	Brown Rice	Strawberries	Pineapple
Brazil Nuts	Wheat	Plums	Banana
Wheat Kernels	Papaya	Blueberries	Mango
Coconut	Stevia & Agave	Raspberries	Walnuts

Most Bottled Water

pH 5.0 — 100x more Acidic

Honey	White Rice	Whole Grain	Rice Cakes
Cooked Beans	Potatoes	Rye Bread	Turbinado Sugar
Bread	Butter-Corn Oil	White Bread	Ketchup &
Liver	Soft Cheeses	White Biscuit	Mayonnaise
Organ Meats	Milk & Cream	Fruit Juice	Figs & Prunes
Cocoa	Cook Tomatoes	Cashews	Rose Hips
Soy Milk	Sweet Potatoes	Oysters	Cooked Corn

Reverse Osmosis Water • Distilled & Purified Waters • Enhanced • Flavored • Vitamin Waters & Sports

pH 4.0 — 1,000x more Acidic

Turkey	Canned Fruits	Peanuts	Coffee
Ocean Fish	Beer & Wines	Pistachios	Chocolate
Chicken & Eggs	Cream Cheese	Fruit Drinks	Cranberries
Hard Cheeses	Most Pastries	Beet Sugar	Buttermilk
Mustard	Popcorn	White Sugar	Tomato Sauce

Carbonated Water • Seltzer or Club Soda

pH 3.0 — 10,000x more Acidic

Pork	Black Tea	Sweetened Fruits & Juices
Veal	Soy Sauce	Stress, Worry, Lack of Sleep
Beef	Hard Liquors	Tobacco Products (Chewed or Smoked)
Lamb	Canned Foods	Artificial Sweeteners (Sweet n' Low, Equal etc.)
Pickles	Processed Foods	16oz. Chocolatty-Mocha-Frappuccinos
Vinegar	Microwaved Foods	SODAS & Carbonated Beverages

Perhaps the ancient mystery schools knew something we didn't know enough about? Thus these cell salts allowed for the body to encode and embody higher frequencies into the body by nourishing the way of the cells. If the body doesn't receive that proper mineral intake, then the cell starts to deplete/dry out if you will. Dating back to the Egyptian era and Greece.

It is safe to say that our body ph has to be evenly balanced for it to work like it should. If more acidity lives within, then you are going to deal with a body that can be easily infected and more supstiple to disease.

So the more you go up in the ph factor, and the more you will improve your overall health. Quite simply put you need to regulate the body, and eat more alkaline foods. With a ph of 7 to 10, which are 1,000 x more alkalinity?

As you can see by the chart beside, the lower you go on the ph factor, the worse your body/temple becomes wrecked with all kinds of nasty parasites, fungus, and other microscopic bacteria that live in all creatures. You are what you eat. The thing is to cut down on the amount of toxins in your body. This is related to your energy centers of the body, the charkas. And if the chakras are in alignment, then you are able to access more of your spiritual power. Also, if you're what I like to call your antenna is working without hardly any interference, then you are able to directly connect with source/God. Drawing in more light. Those walk with light, walk with God? But let me remind you that there are over 1,000's of other different spiritual practices all over this great nation! It's what works best for you. Most of our issues stem from being out of balance with the chakras, thus it creates problems and energy blocks. This is why we acupuncture for. No surprise there, what are they always trying to accomplish by pushing pens into you? To unblock the blocked energy. If the energy isn't in synch with the body, the energy isn't flowing properly. And once that happens, you have all kinds of symptoms of fatigue, loss of energy, less vibrant feeling. More like run down, overworked, stressed out and under paid! Lol. What I am trying to get at is, you have all this issues all the sudden arise, your back, your legs, or quite possibly could be a pain in your neck. Whatever it is, well...There is certainly a reason for it. So, how does one go about keeping the body working without mishaps? Without getting sicker quicker? Well . . . what we are dealing with is every day toxins that are always around us or in our space. So you first have to figure out to what degree you need to pay attention to your body and what it needs and has to have to function properly.

We are always looking for a quick fix!

Always looking for the pill to fix what is wrong with us. Why do you think about it being permanent when in fact it's only temporary? What it all boils down to is being consciously aware about what's going on around you at all times. Yes, I mean be vigilant with your health. I have watched countless of people go down the hill before they were ever suppose to. I watched my families' health deteriorate at a much quicker pace verse the ratio of time to decay process that takes place naturally as you begin the aging process. The body breaks down at a much accelerated pace if it were not to get the suitable diet or overall balanced for life dedication to you and it. How is it we could have lived 200 years once upon a time ago? Perhaps they knew nature's secrets to longetivity? Perhaps they pay more attention to the cycles and seasons of life. More connected to the cosmos? I think over time it has become apparent that we, as people don't pay attention to those things that matter anymore, and then we fall out of synch with life and nature herself, thus our bodies suffer for our inactions. But let's not forget that the mind & soul needs nourishment too. Without tending to a garden, it results in weeds. Same thing happens when spiritual neglect happens, the soul recedes!

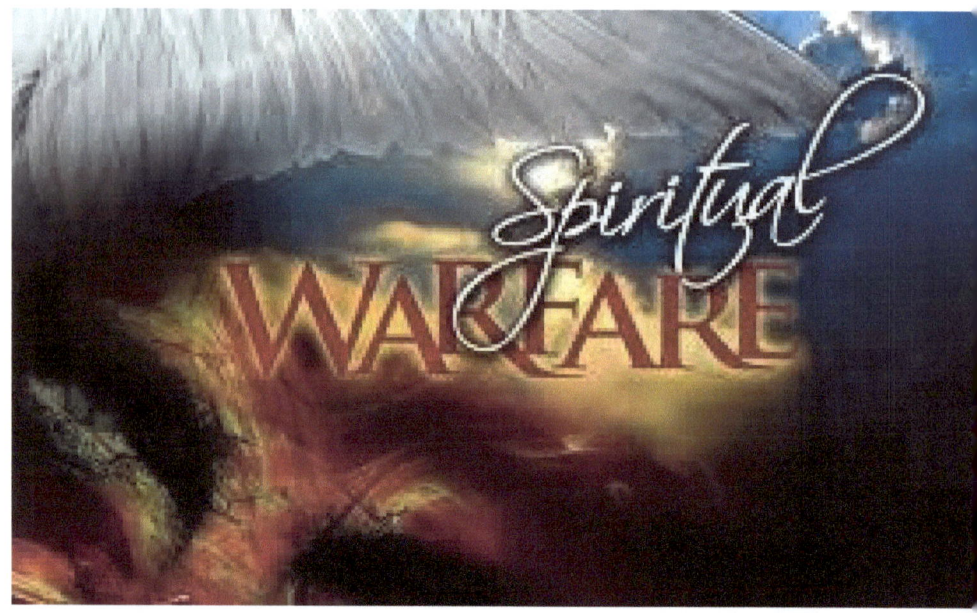

Chakras and Stones

7th, Crown: *Subtle element: Intelligence.* God consciousness, spiritual intelligence

Moonstone, selenite, crystal quartz, amethyst

6th, Brow: *Subtle element: Mind.* Inner vision, intuition, comprehension

Iolite, lapis lazuli, labradorite, sapphire

5th, Throat: *Element: Ether.* Communication, expression, higher will

Turquoise, apatite

4th, Heart: *Element: Air.* Love, surrender, balance, acceptance, devotion

Rose quartz, emerald, peridot

3rd, Solar Plexus: *Element: Fire.* Will, personal power, perseverance, confidence

Citrine, topaz, tiger's eye

2nd, Sacral: *Element: Water.* Physical vitality, desire, creativity, passion

Coral, Carnelian, pearl

1st, Root: *Element: Earth.* Physical body, survival, past impressions

Garnet, ruby, hematite, onyx, jasper

7 CHAKRAS FOR BEGINNERS

Crown Chakra
Problems: issues with sleep/wake cycle, feeling disconnected from your body or others, difficulty meditating, spiritual discomfort

Solutions: fresh air, sunlight, nature

Third Eye
Problems: depression, poor eyesight, hormonal imbalances, poor intuition

Foods: purple potatoes, blackberries, plums, purple grapes

Throat Chakra
Problems: thyroid disease, frequent sore throat, difficulty expressing feelings

Foods: blueberries, blue raspberries, figs, kelp

Heart Chakra
Problems: heart and lung problems, asthma, allergies, fear of intimacy

Foods: broccoli, kale, chard, all other leafy greens

Solar Plexus Chakra
Problems: gas, bloating, liver issues, stomach ulcers, eating disorders, lack of confidence, procrastination

Foods: yellow peppers, yellow lentils, yellow squash, oats, spelt

Sacral Chakra
Problems: infertility, hip pain, sexual dysfunction, emotional imbalances, creative blocks

Foods: seeds, nuts, oranges, carrots, pumpkins

Root Chakra
Problems: colon issues, lower back pain, varicose veins, emotional issues surrounding money and security

Foods: beets, parsnips, rutabaga, apples, pomegranates, protein

Something inside breaks and cracks starts to form within your being. You feel a change must come. It has to there can be no other way. You work hard for the day that the light makes it way traveling up to the surface. You know why you made the choice in the first place. You wanted to show the world or your family who you really are inside. The hurt only drives you to want that success even more! There is only the way we all know in our hearts to be true. Never let them tell you who to be. Never let them tell you what you can achieve. I am living proof that you can do anything, be anything and beat the odds!

In all honesty, I believe that hard work does pay off, and so what if others can't see the work you're putting in. Remember one thing... It all comes back full circle. You get what you give; you reap what you sew, so sew & weave good... Sew something that WOWs everyone and makes them take notice. You did work for it after all. Take a bow... And smile. You made it!

I think we all hold the world in our hands and hearts. How much do you want the world to change? How much do you put into making that change happen? Aren't you powerful?

I can't even begin to tell you how much meditation can help center your awareness or even give you clarity where there was none prior. My thing is this, close your eyes and just imagine, visualize and picture yourself somewhere other than the current situation you find you are presently in. After all, we are going for the end-result.

Ready to take a little trip?

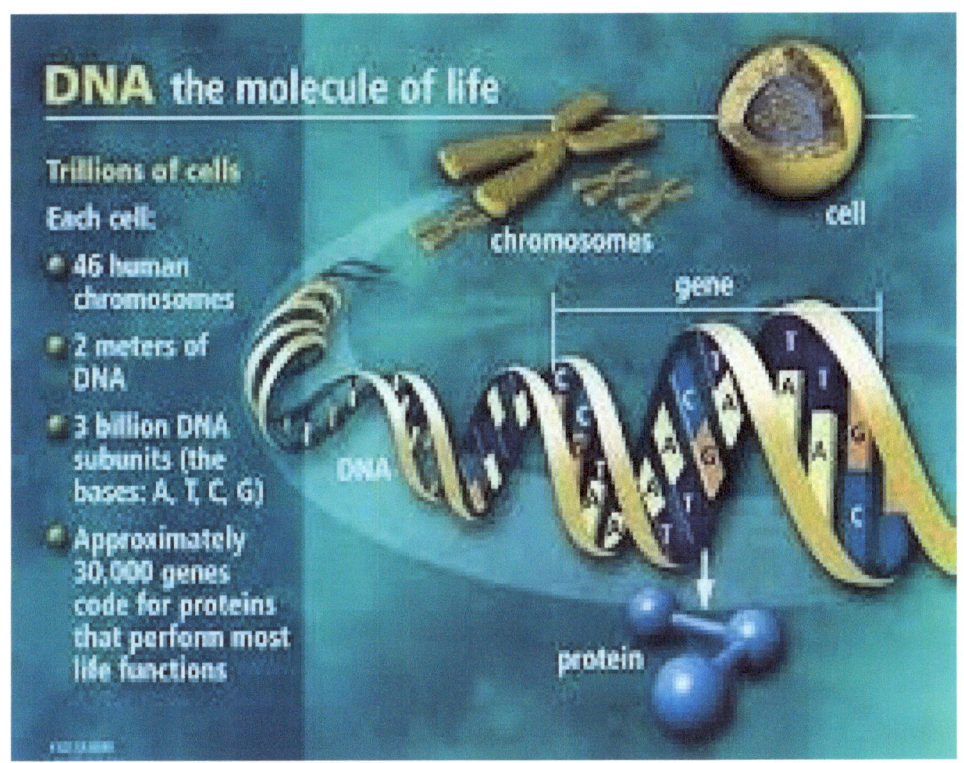

The blueprint for all life on Earth. How you evolve really is determined by your code within your DNA. What have you programmed yours for?

Your thoughts have a lot to do with how much information your DNA/antenna can receive. How fast you heal. Also what kind of stuff you're feeding it. Is it pure energy? If you are energy then why not feed it what it so deliciously deserves? What does DNA crave? How about it craves to uncoil and live up to its full potential. What if it only needed light codes and sound to do this? It's been proven that music can alter it. That it changes your way of thinking. Also, the music can do much more than to just be therapeutic, it can open up to receive more information when it's not bunched together. For when DNA is in its natural state, let say love state, then it's able to hit on more areas of the strand of DNA. In a fear state, it's as if the DNA retreats and coils in on itself. Why do you think they call it a higher frequency? Why do you think they say fear is the lowest dense energy? Because it is! Let me purpose to say that if you are in a constant state of fear than you can't possible tap into what is known as the higher/evolved self.

All life is created from love, or there had to be something to create life as you and I know. It had to form from a thought, a gleam in your parent's eyes to create you. Consciousness/thought creates the world in which we all co-exist in. I don't believe there is such a thing as bad genetics, after what I have thus figured out so far. I think it has to deal in bad choices, especially in the health department. You either don't put crap into your vessel or you do. You either make a decision to help someone in need or you don't. See.... It all boils down to the choices we make in this one life we all have a chance to share and learn/grow from. I am a firm believer in karma though. You get what give! And if you are carrying other frequencies, energies from others, then you are weighed down. There is such a thing as energy vampires. Yes, they do feed on the lower life forms. How would you even know what one of these beings looks like? I will tell you... after being around one, you will know because your vibrant energy will be drained completely. The phase "I feel like a truck ran over me." Fits this, not only because it's true but that is exactly the feeling you get from being around this kind of person/individual.

When you get away from those kinds of energies that are draining your energy, you then are able to emit your own frequency and come into your own. They aren't hitching a ride on you anymore. Being around people that will lift you up in life is what you need to be around. The Go Getters, the ones that are there to the end. Those are a bit harder to find though. Once you find your kind, tribe it becomes much easier to get along in life. Not everyone you come across has the best intentions for you.

Smudging is a good way to clear out unwanted and negative energy.

She is reaching for her other half; perhaps her higher self is reaching to help her from the other side. Does she reach back and take the hand that is being offered? We all need help in life sometimes. As you see she is coming more into focus, and less faded out as the hand is a healing hand that is making her whole again.

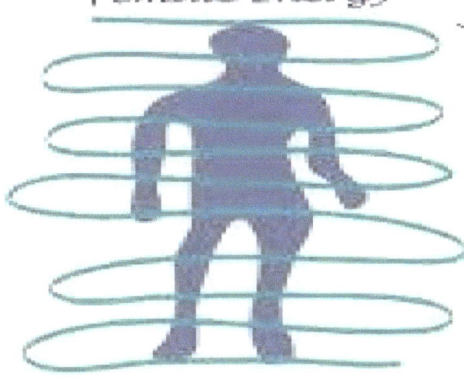

FEMALE (Right Brain) Characteristics	MALE (Left Brain) Characteristics
circular	hierarchical
being	doing
surrender	aggression
wholistic thinking	analytical/sequential thinking
abstract conceptualization	concrete conceptualization
patience	impatience
tranquility	striving
nurturing	rushing
recieving (like a cupped hand)	aggressive/thrusting (like a sword)
spontaneous/synthesizing	incremental
emotional	logical
creative	analytical
intuitive	mathematical
calm	busy
soft	hard
allowing	controlling

Female energies:
- Intuition
- Nurturing
- Healing
- Calm
- Emotional awareness
- Expression and communication of emotions

Male energies:
- Logic
- Reason
- Energy of action
- Firm
- Ease of acquiring material needs
- Survival
- Common sense

Each soul, person seeks to balance these energies to become a whole being. To become aware of these energies and be able to utilize them when they are needed.

The repression of the divine feminine has led the planet on the edge and verge of total collapse. The re-emergence is going to be something that will have you on the edge of your seat, a dance that will be something to behold!

When we are in nature, we are in our natural state. In our element ~ that's why it feels so joyful, a state of inexplicable bliss…

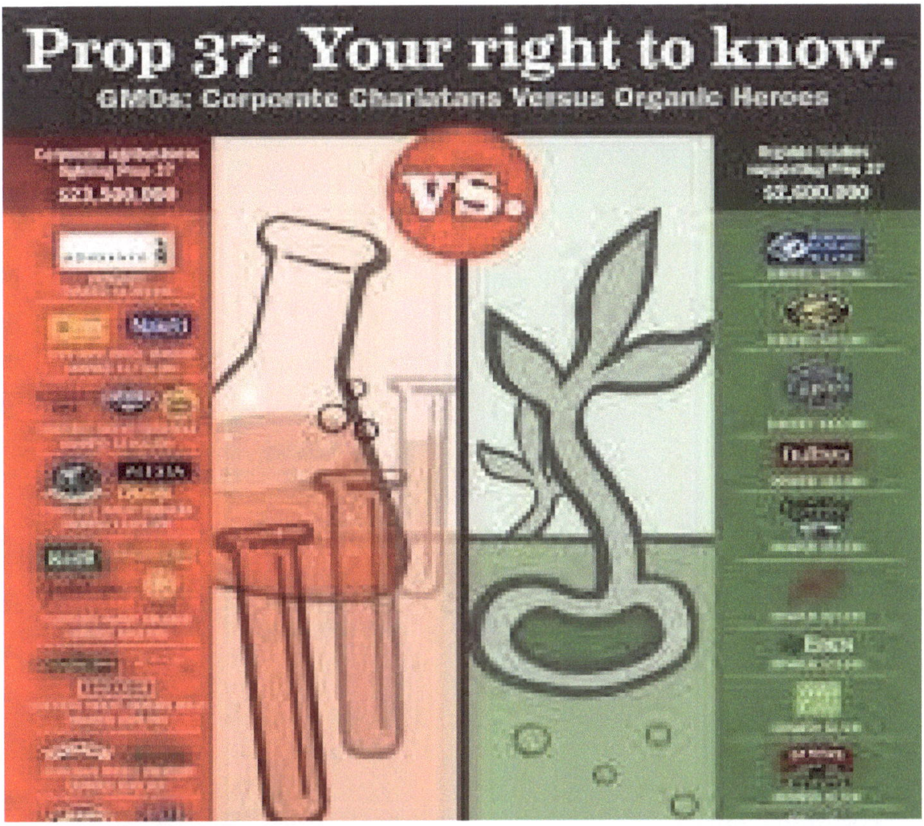
Prop 37: Your right to know.
GMOs: Corporate Charlatans Versus Organic Heroes
VS.

INFINITE LOVE
IS THE ONLY TRUTH

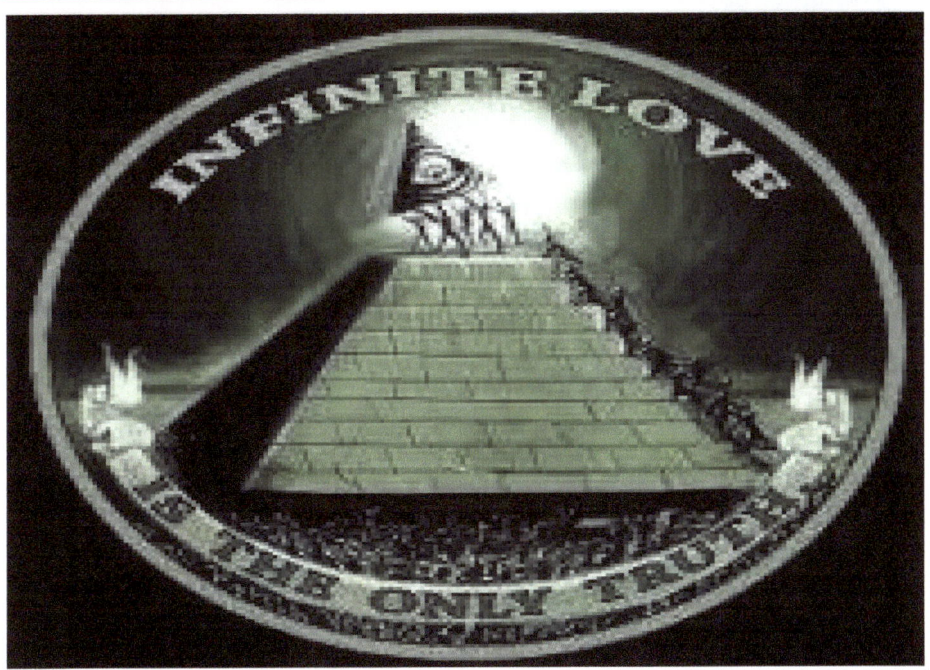

KUNDALINI AWAKENING
THIRD EYE

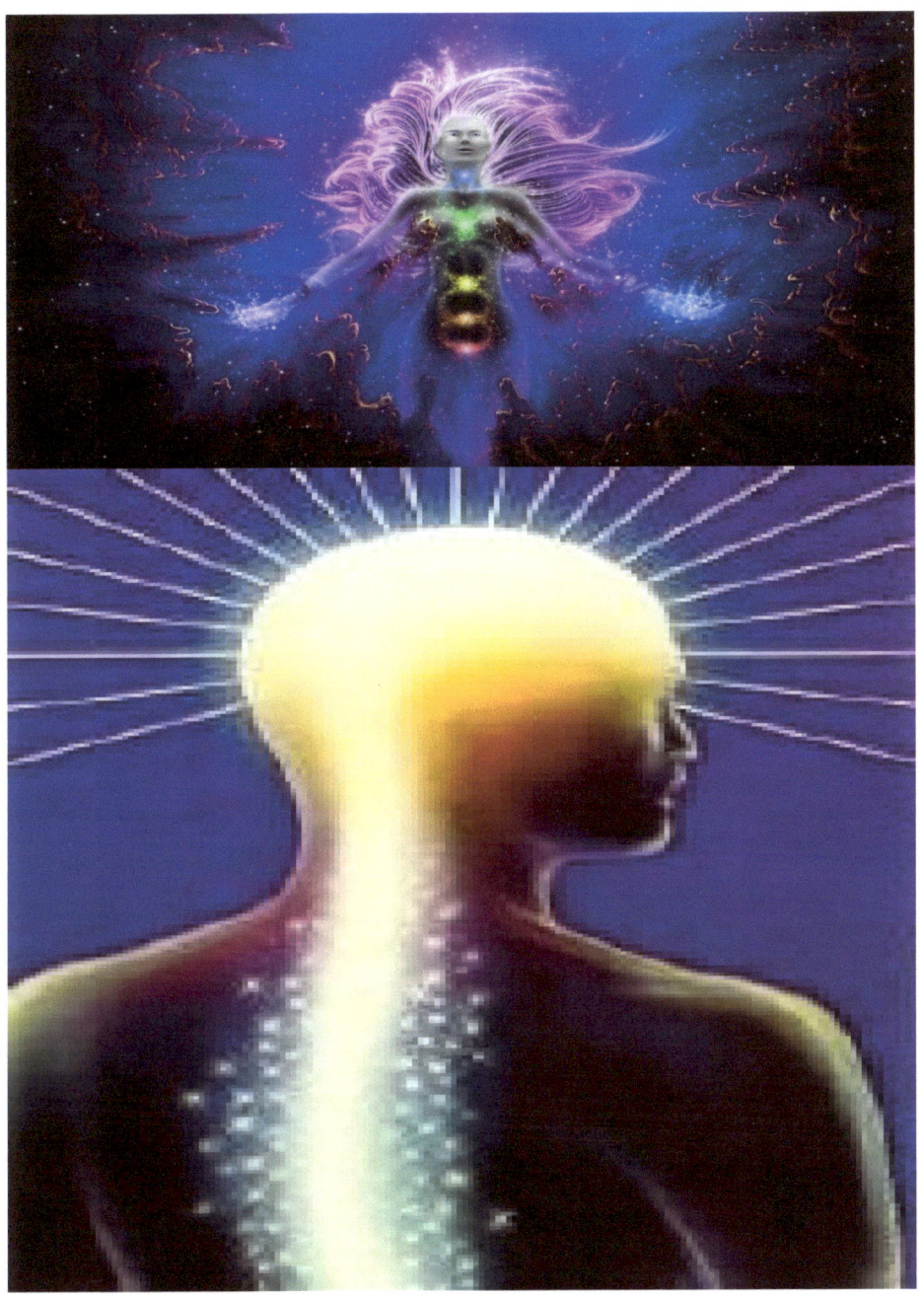

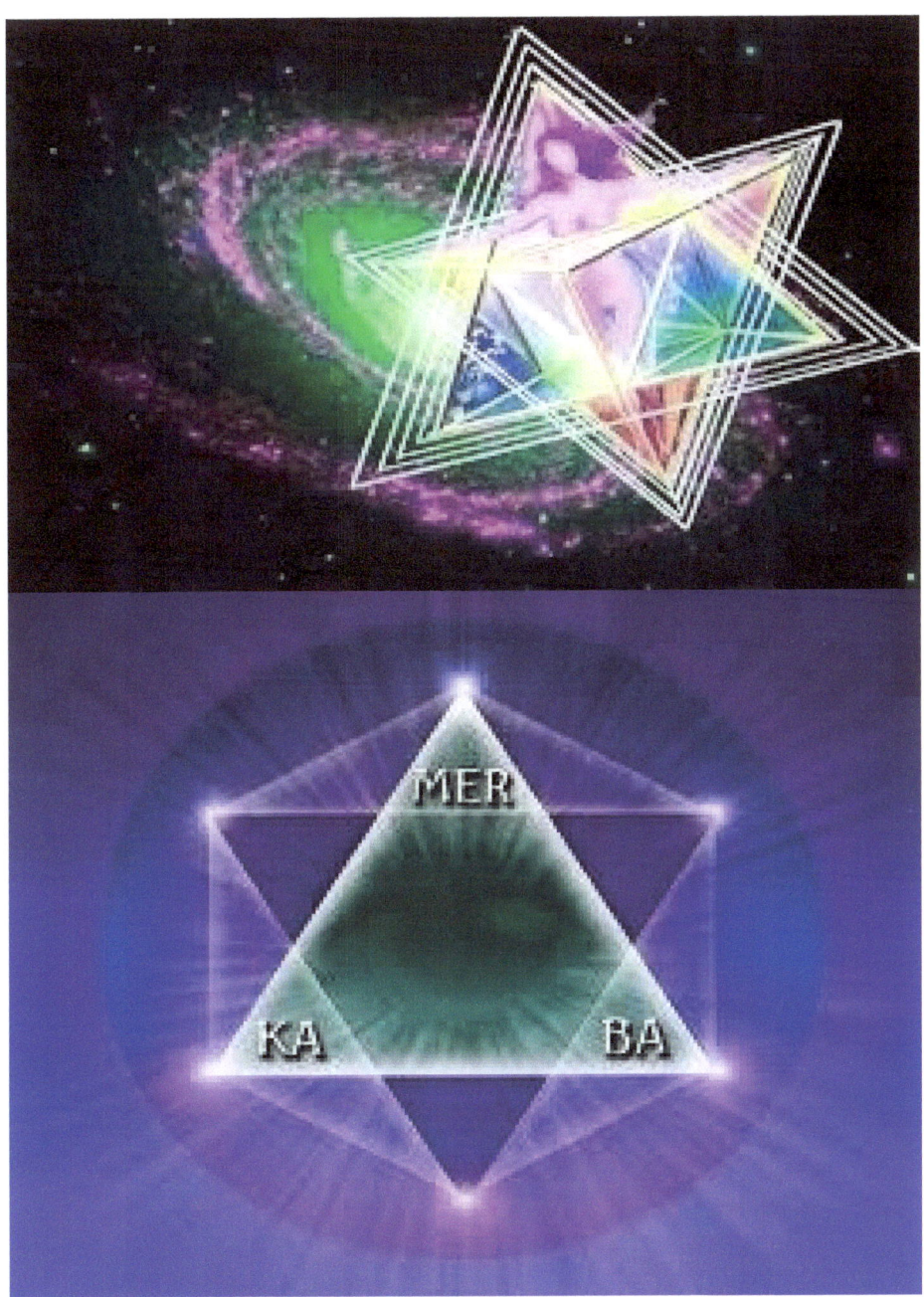

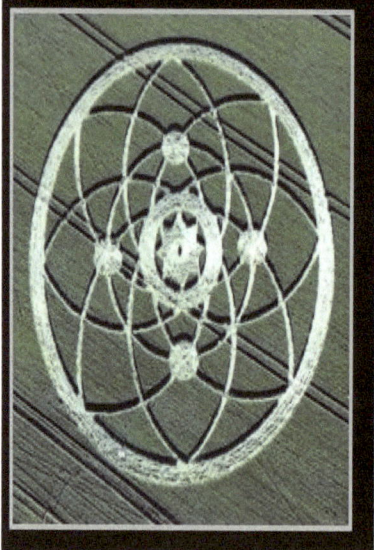

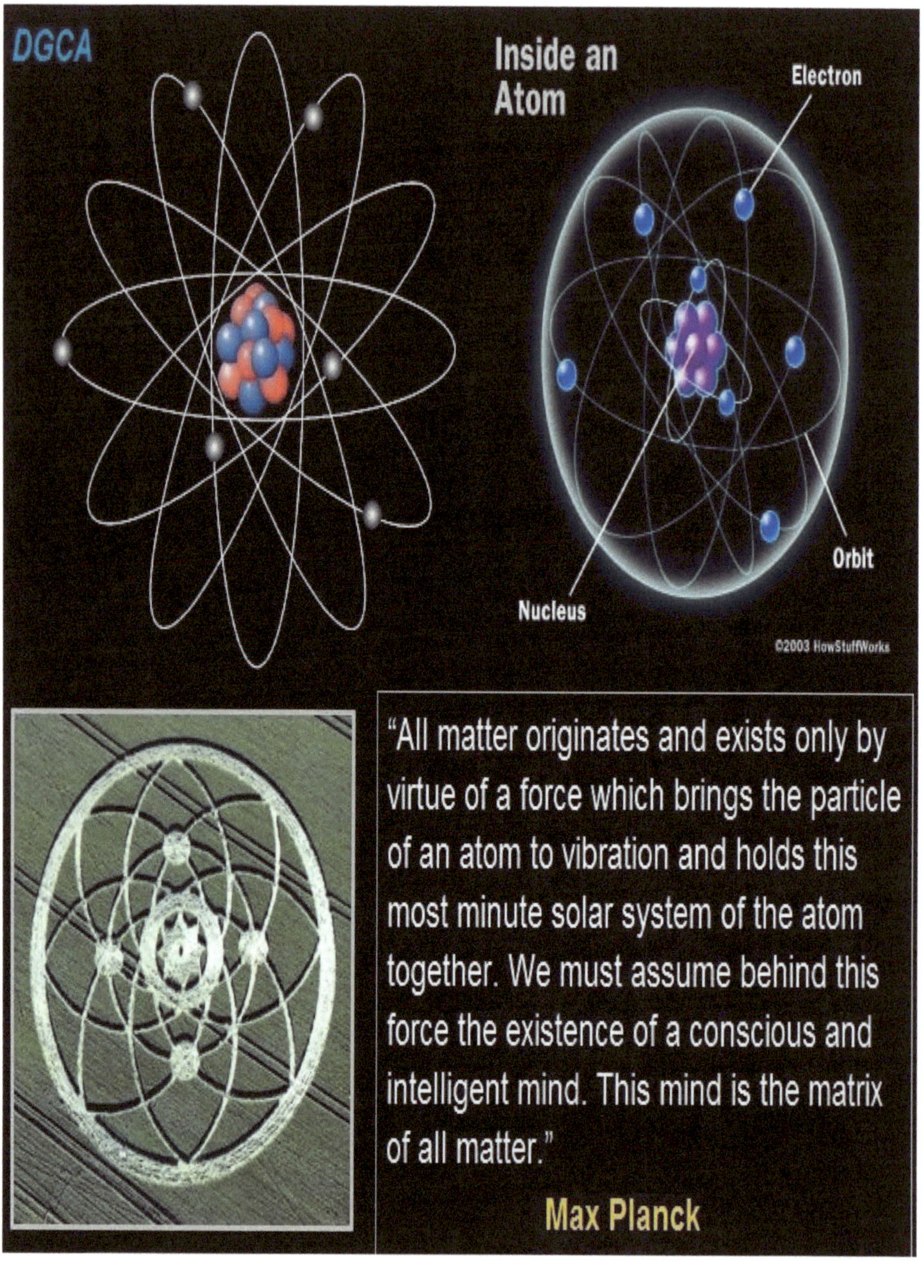
DGCA
Inside an Atom
Electron
Orbit
Nucleus
©2003 HowStuffWorks
“All matter originates and exists only by virtue of a force which brings the particle of an atom to vibration and holds this most minute solar system of the atom together. We must assume behind this force the existence of a conscious and intelligent mind. This mind is the matrix of all matter.”
Max Planck

PLANNING FOR GROWTH, INVESTING IN OUR FUTURE

 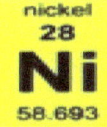  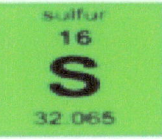

Exceptional intellectual or creative power or other natural ability. A person who is exceptionally intelligent or creative, either generally or in some particular respect.

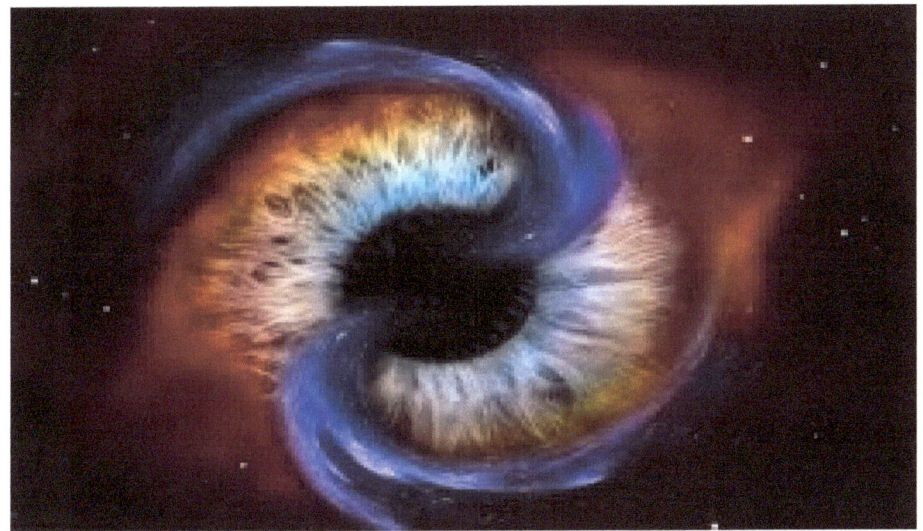

Goddess

~ A woman that is in the process of learning to know, accept and love herself on all levels; Mind, Body and Spirit.

~ A woman who, because she focuses on personal growth and self awareness, experiences a life increasingly filled with peace, love, joy, passion and fun.

~ A woman that understands that she has an unlimited capacity to make her life anything she wants.

~ A woman who is inspired to give to those around her out of her sense of gratitude and abundance.

I've found the Goddess in myself.

I love her fiercely...

So, I am here to tell you that the Revolution of the Divine Feminine is here to stay! Never let them take that power YOU hold away. Show them what you're made of; show them what's on the inside, where it counts!

We are no less than the trees, the land, the wind, water and fire. Earth calls for our help, she beckons for us to awaken and take care of her and the children. She whispers... Keeping your feet firmly planted on the ground. Even when inspiration has seemed to have left me, it somehow has a way of making itself come back around. Standing in moral code. My compass for life's eternal gage.

My sacred heart... I will never forsake thee...

Books to come: 2016 - 2022

Through The Looking Glass

Gods & Goddesses

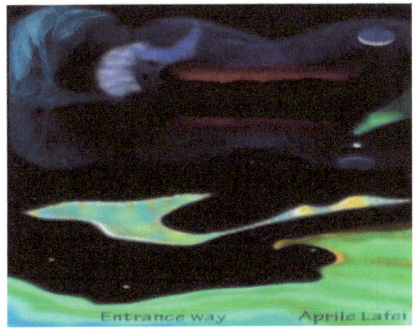

Given Wings to Fly

Books to come: 2016 - 2022

Secrets of the Heart

Rebirth of the Goddess

Through the Cracks

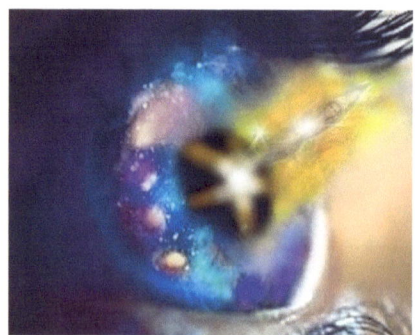

Book to come: 2016 - 2022
Star Nations

Revolutionary Uprising

Children of the Sun

www.ingramcontent.com/pod-product-compliance
Lightning Source LLC
Chambersburg PA
CBHW041622220426
43662CB00001B/17